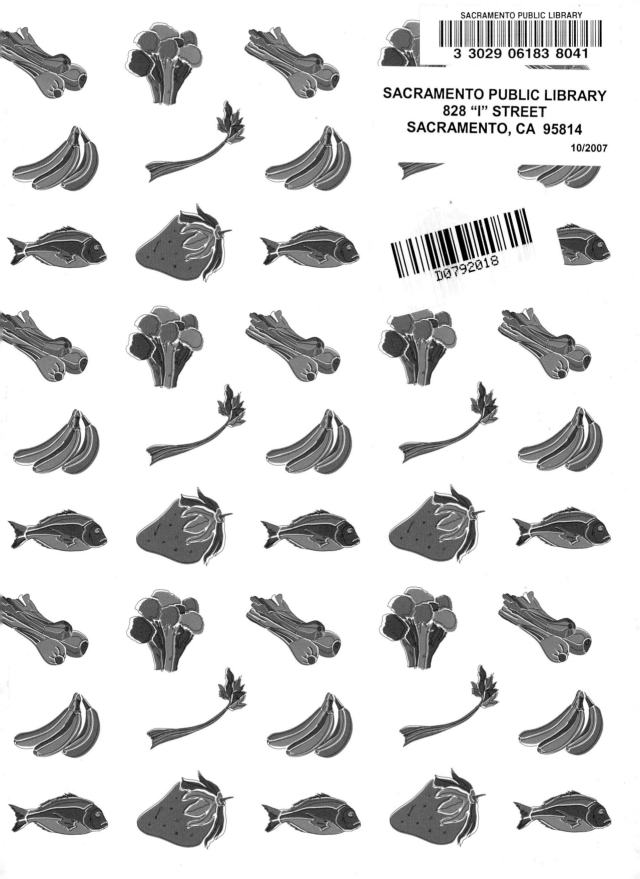

THE TRUTH ABOUT FOOD

WHAT YOU EAT CAN CHANGE YOUR LIFE

JILL FULLERTON-SMITH

WITH A FOREWORD BY

MEHMET C. OZ, M.D.,
COAUTHOR OF
YOU: THE OWNER'S MANUAL

B L O O M S B U R Y

**For my daughter Billie and my stepchildren,
Michael, Corrina, Alex and Charlie.**

Design and Art Direction: Caz Hildebrand, Here+There
Copy editors: Sarah Hall, James Kingsland
Indexer: Vanessa Bird

Food illustrations: Dan Bernstein
Food photographs: Andy Grimshaw
Science images: Science Photo Library 32, (Steve Gschmeissner); 72,142
(Susumu Nishinaga); 103 (Omikron); 165, 225 (Omnikron); 185 (CNRI);
202 (Dr. John Zajicek)

Discovery Health Channel and the Discovery Health Channel logo are
trademarks of Discovery Communications, Inc., used under license.

Published by Bloomsbury USA, New York
Distributed to the trade by Holtzbrinck Publishers

All papers used by Bloomsbury USA are natural, recyclable products made
from wood grown in well-managed forests. The manufacturing processes
conform to the environmental regulations of the country of origin.

LIBRARY OF CONGRESS CATALOGING-IN-PUBLICTION DATA HAS BEEN APPLIED FOR

ISBN-10: 1-59691-267-7
ISBN-13: 978-1-59691-267-0

First U.S. Edition 2007

1 3 5 7 9 10 8 6 4 2

Printed in Hong Kong, China by C&C Offset Printing

Foreword

Few relationships in our lives are more rewarding, frustrating, intimate or important than our bond with food. From our earliest days, when our nourishment comes with the warm closeness of a parent's gentle touch and whispered endearments, we associate food with comfort and satisfaction. Throughout our lives, mealtimes are so much more than simply eating: they often can be moments of sharing pieces of ourselves with those we care about. In virtually every society, breaking bread together is an important cultural symbol, a time when we welcome others into our circle.

If food were merely fuel, we could consume a simple, tasteless liquid and be on our way, just as we fill up our cars with gasoline to keep us on the road. But nothing about food is simple. Even the most basic signals that tell us we are hungry or full are confused by a host of psychological and physiological triggers that often make it difficult for us to identify when we need to eat or—more importantly for most of us—when we need to stop eating.

In a society where food is plentiful, diverse, quick and relatively cheap, it's no wonder that our nation is waging a collective battle against obesity and a host of associated diseases. It's hard to resist food's many temptations. As a cardiothoracic surgeon, I see the effects of diet on my patients every day. Heart disease, stroke and diabetes are mostly linked to lifestyle choices.

The good news, though, is that our bodies are surprisingly forgiving and elastic. By changing the foods we select and how much we eat, we can often reduce or eliminate the effects of years of dietary abuse. But how do you know which are the "right" and "wrong" foods for you? Are there such things as "bad" foods? The media inundate us daily with stories about the winners and losers in the food roulette, and today misinformation can spread faster than ever before. Even good scientific research suggesting a positive effect of a single food can be blown up in the press and become a fad.

Coming up with a sensible food plan that not only works, but is one you can live with, is a daunting task. If eating a healthy diet and staying slim were easy, we would all do it. The challenges have as much to do with our hearts as our heads, and any time our hearts are involved, life gets complicated.

Can food make us smarter, thinner, faster, younger, sexier and healthier? Yes, indeed. It can also make us fatter, slower, older and sicker. Because we hear so much about food in our daily lives and battle with it daily, we think we know a great deal. In truth, much of what we "know" about food isn't true at all.

The Truth About Food offers us enlightening experiments, based on larger clinical studies, that help clear up common misconceptions about food and offer intriguing evidence that foods can be as powerful as pharmaceuticals in improving health and well-being. From an experiment in which people significantly reduced their blood pressure and cholesterol simply by changing their diet to a demonstration showing that merely eating soup before a meal can make you feel fuller longer while consuming fewer calories, the experiments described here offer convincing evidence in support of the power of food to enhance life. Foods are powerful weapons in our fight to stay healthy. Use them well. *The Truth About Food* offers you valuable information on how to do just that.

Mehmet C. Oz, M.D.
Director, Cardiovascular Institute
and Vice Chairman, Department of Surgery,
Columbia University Medical Center;
Professor of Surgery,
Columbia University College of Physicians and Surgeons

Contents

INTRODUCTION

Why does your best friend eat like a horse and look like a gazelle? And why does your sister feel full after a sandwich while you still feel peckish after a three-course meal? Do carrots really improve your eyesight or would spinach be nearer the mark? Can the foods you eat really affect your libido or increase your fertility? Does your son reject his vegetables because he's a fussy eater, or is it because his taste buds are different from his sister's?

For answers to questions like these, look no further than *The Truth About Food*. This book accompanies a major television series of the same name, which I conceived and produced. It took two years of hard work to make. There are six programs in the series – each chapter of this book reflects the content from one of the programs.

The Truth About Food reveals the real science of food using the latest research from leaders in the field of nutrition, alongside original and sometimes groundbreaking experiments that we carried out especially for the series. We worked with more than fifty nutritionists, doctors and other experts from more than twenty different universities, research centers and hospitals in the UK, the USA and Denmark. We used a total of more than 500 volunteers in our experiments.

Toni Egger from Discovery Channel helped frame the series and her advice was invaluable. Many of the ideas were developed with Alon Orstein, our executive producer from the Discovery Health team.

Throughout the book are boxes labeled "Top Tips." These have been specially designed as practical ways for you to apply the scientific ideas contained in the book. In some cases, they allow you to replicate diets followed by our experiment volunteers. Of course, the advice and information in this book is not a substitute for individual, professional advice about diet and health. In particular, those with specific medical conditions should consult their doctor or a registered dietician.

When I started working with Discovery Channel seven years ago as a producer and director of scientific programs, I was captivated by the breakthroughs in molecular biology – the study of the inner workings of our bodies. I developed a passion for science and its potential to change our lives, and that passion became the driving force behind this book and the television series that came before it.

While making the programs, I found my own attitudes toward food were changing. I began to think more about what I was eating, and what it could do for me. I began to plan meals, and take more notice of food labels in the supermarket. I realized that food is absolutely fascinating. I hope that reading this book – and, if you also caught the series, watching the programs – will have a similar effect on you.

Today, food is a key talking point, a source of controversy and an important issue in our daily lives. We read magazine articles about food, watch television programs, buy diet books and, if we want to know more, there's always the Internet. Not a week passes without one food-related issue or another making the headlines – whether it's a debate over labeling regulations or the latest celebrity diet. And three times a day, almost every day of our lives, we eat. We eat to live – but we also eat to celebrate, to relieve boredom, to commiserate, to socialize, to beat illness, to de-stress, to bulk up or to slim down.

Long ago, our relationship with food was far simpler; food was about survival, and life revolved around the search for food. It was quite literally a matter of life and death. While this is still the case in some parts of many developing countries today, here in the Western world few of us live more than a short drive from the nearest supermarket with its heaving shelves and vast range of shiny new products. We have never had greater choice, with food imported from every corner of the globe, and we've never been better informed about food. So what's gone wrong – why aren't we all healthy, fit and trim?

One of the biggest problems is dealing with the sheer volume of information out there. Understanding complex research can be hard going; experts disagree; journalists speculate; and old myths die hard. The result is confusion, and even a fear of food – a very modern phenomenon. It seems the more we know, the more we have to worry about, and the less sure we are of the truth. We worry about additives, preservatives, eating disorders, hygiene, heart disease, cancer and calories. We worry about what we are feeding our children and the global consequences of what we eat. Little wonder it's tempting to seize upon the latest fad or celebrity edict.

Food is fundamental for all human beings, yet we are only just starting to understand how it affects our bodies, and why people react differently to different foods. This puts food at the scientific cutting-edge. Leading the field are a few teams of top molecular biologists, who are beginning to unravel the mysterious ways in which food affects us. One of the biggest breakthroughs they have made is the revelation that the desire for food – our appetite – is hard-wired, for the simple reason that this drive once ensured our survival when food was scarce.

Now, it seems, our genetic desire to eat is conspiring against us. I wondered if simple hunger is the reason why so many diets fail. And then it hit me: if feeling hungry is part of our genetic makeup, then surely the sensation of feeling full must also be a biological signal. What tells the body "I am no longer hungry?" It must be food. What if there were some foods that could keep us feeling full for longer. I was hooked.

I quickly discovered that powerful drug companies around the world are also racing to work out what happens to food in the hidden microscopic world of our cells, our blood and our brains. With huge sums of money at stake, their holy grail is a safe pill to stop our appetite. They believe this pill would be more successful than Viagra – and the many women who think about food as often as men are said to think about sex would probably agree.

The aim of this book is to move away from a culture of pill popping, and discover the foods that not only help us to control our appetite, but also fight aging, boost happiness, improve memory or increase fertility. It's about replacing the confusion and fear that surrounds food with an understanding of its positive potential.

Can you really eat to be thin? Or eat to stay young, be smarter or happier? You become the scientist, your body the subject.

Jill Fullerton-Smith

The digestive system:
taking what you need

You probably have drawn and labeled a diagram of the digestive system at least once while you were at school. For those of you who need a refresher, here is a quick summary of how each organ plays a part in the process of taking nutrients from your food and delivering them to your body.

When you put food into your mouth, your teeth chew, your salivary glands spurt saliva. As a result, your food gets mashed up and made into a soft ball called a bolus.

When you swallow, your tongue pushes the bolus down the esophagus **(1)** – a long muscular tube that leads down to the stomach **(2)**. The bolus is moved down by waves of muscle action. There is a valve at the entrance to the stomach, which opens to allow the food to enter.

The stomach is basically a bag of muscle. It can normally hold up to 1.5 liters (3 pints) of food. The strong acid and other digestive juices are added to the bolus to facilitate breakdown of complex molecules of protein, fat and carbohydrate into small, more absorbable units. The mixture – now called chyme – remains in the stomach for between forty minutes and a few hours.

There is a small, round muscle – called the pylorus – located at the outlet of the stomach. When the pylorus opens, it allows the chyme into the small intestine, which is between 4.5 and 6 meters (15 to 20 feet) long. It is here that most nutrients are absorbed into the body. The small intestine is made up of three sections.

In the duodenum **(3)**, the chyme is mixed with bile and digestive juices from the pancreas **(4)**. Bile is a greenish liquid produced by the liver and stored in the gall bladder **(5)** between meals. It dissolves fats into the water, so that they can be absorbed. Iron and calcium is absorbed in the duodenum.

The jejunum **(6)** is the second and longest part of the small intestine. It is here that the majority of the broken-down nutrients pass into the body. Most are carried in the blood, which passes straight to the liver **(7)**, where it is filtered and detoxified. Fats pass into the lymphatic system, for filtering and further processing, before being introduced into the blood. The last segment of the intestine, the ileum **(8)**, is where the absorption of fat-soluble vitamins A, D, E and K and other nutrients takes place.

The mixture now passes into the large intestine **(9)**, where water is absorbed, and where billions of bacteria break down some of the otherwise indigestible carbohydrates (soluble fiber). Anything left that cannot be digested, along with dead blood cells that were contained in bile, is stored in the large intestine, passing along slowly until it reaches the rectum **(10)**. When the rectum is full, it is time to visit the toilet. Feces are pushed out through the anus **(11)**.

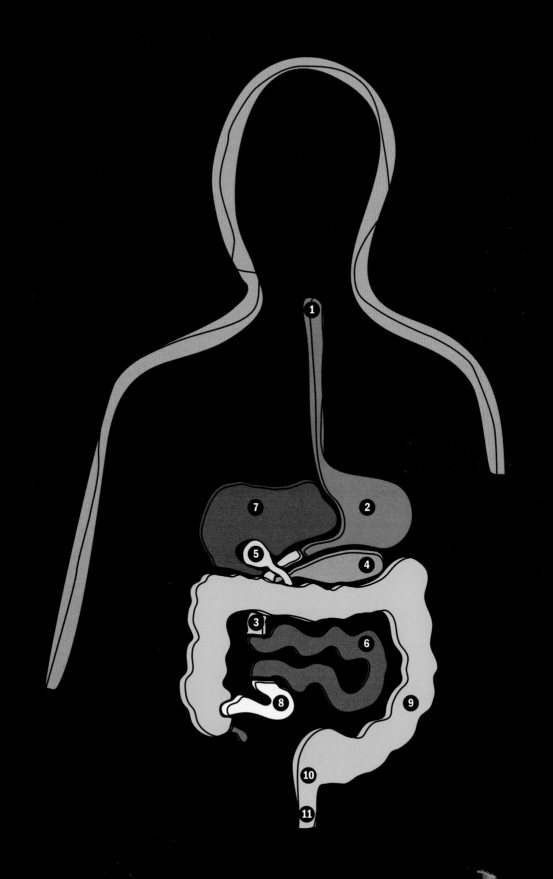

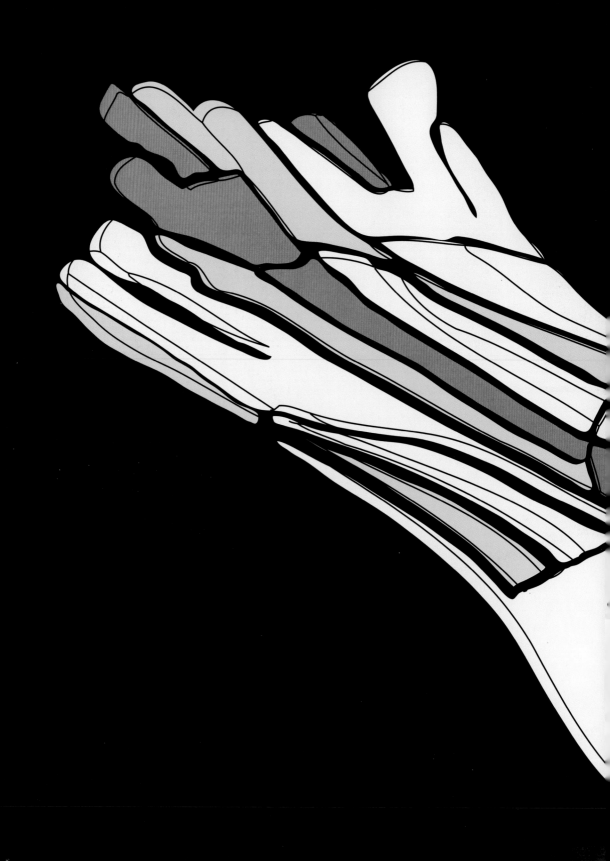

1. HOW TO BE HEALTHY

HOW TO BE HEALTHY

In the fight for health, it's pretty clear which foods are on which side. In the left corner, looking trim and bouncing around, raring to go, are five-a-day fruits and vegetables, high-fiber breads, low-fat yogurts. In the right corner, fat and sweaty and already out of breath, are chips, burgers and fries, processed cheese, white bread.

But what separates the winners from the losers? What exactly is going on inside the body? Why are porridge oats and broccoli so good for you, soft drinks and ice cream so bad? With our experts on board, we embarked on a journey to discover the optimum healthy diet.

The first clues that diet affects our health come from epidemiology, the study of the links between lifestyle, the environment and disease. By comparing the lifestyles of people in different countries, for example, epidemiologists can identify factors that contribute to a host of diseases.

Of course, not all diseases are food-related: smoking, stress and pollution are also major factors, as are the genes we're born with. But hundreds of studies strongly suggest that the high-fat, high-sugar, low-fiber Western diet is a major factor in heart disease, diabetes and cancer.

What effects could different foods be having inside the body to put us at risk from, or protect us from, such terrible diseases? The human body is very good at fighting disease all on its own, but it needs the right supplies at the front line. The main lines of defense are the immune system, the liver and colonies of good bacteria in our intestines. So what kind of supplies do they need?

We looked at the role of dietary fiber – something lacking in the typical Western diet of today. Fiber seems to play at least two important roles in helping our bodies keep us healthy. First, it feeds the colonies of beneficial bacteria living in our large intestines. Second, there is evidence that a diet high in fiber can help to prevent a major killer, colon cancer. We investigated both of these ideas – we even sent a camera on a trip through the digestive system, to see if we could find out more.

The body has a sophisticated system for dealing with toxins, but some people worry that in the modern world, we can become overloaded with harmful substances. "Detoxing" – attempting to cleanse our bodies of toxins – offers the chance to stay healthy despite living in the modern, toxin-filled world. We set out to see if detox programs can really deliver what they promise.

The temporary discomfort we feel after overdosing on popular recreational toxins like alcohol pales into insignificance when compared with some of the truly life-threatening challenges to human health. Medical science has conquered many of the biggest killers in the developed world – for example cholera and smallpox. So, in the West at least, there is more emphasis on "chronic" (long-term) diseases such as heart disease and cancer.

Scientists have discovered a chemical in broccoli that seems to protect against cancer. The effect of this chemical varies between people, depending upon their genetic makeup. In fact, there are many genes that determine how "healthy" or "unhealthy" a particular food will be, and they vary between individuals. In the future, genetic testing might be used to give everyone his or her own recommendations for a healthy diet.

The Evo Diet:
eat like your ancestors

Beef burgers, lovingly sandwiched between two halves of a white bread roll. French fries and soft drinks – why not "go large"? Chocolate and ice cream for dessert. Tasty foods like these make us feel good in the short term. But eat them most of the time and they can increase blood pressure and cholesterol, recognized by the majority of doctors as the most important factors in heart disease and stroke – the world's biggest killers.

Current medical wisdom suggests that if you lower your cholesterol and your blood pressure, you will significantly reduce your chance of suffering from heart disease. And it can be done. Millions of people – many of them in the USA – take drugs called statins that reduce levels of "bad" cholesterol by up to a third. And there are also medicines that reduce blood pressure.

But you can reduce cholesterol and blood pressure without using drugs. According to some scientists, you just have to say no to the junk food and sugary snacks – and eat the same as our distant ancestors.

Evolution "designed" the human body long ago, when people didn't eat ice cream, chocolate and French fries. Early humans kept no medical records, but archaeologists can tell what they ate – and what they died from – with surprising accuracy. What our ancestors ate may hold the key to discovering the healthiest diet. Keen to play our part in this quest for the ideal nosh, we asked a group of junk-food-loving volunteers to try out the diet of their distant ancestors, to see whether it would improve their vital signs.

Origin of the species

Modern humans have been around for a very long time. Our species – *Homo sapiens* – originated on the African savannah nearly 200,000 years ago. In evolutionary terms, that's a blink of the eye, so there are very few substantial genetic differences between you and the people who lived then.

So, take yourself back about 10,000 generations and meet your ancestors. It is 180,000 BC. All the humans in existence live on the African savannah. There are obviously no shops – but there is also no farming. People don't even herd animals. The men hunt and fish, the women gather food and look after the children. These people's diets are not very different from their more hairy human-like predecessors – nor for that matter is their digestive system. Like the rest of the body, the digestive system has evolved very gradually.

How can we be so sure what our prehistoric ancestors ate? They didn't leave menus or food packaging lying around. Instead, archaeologists examine fossilized feces, called coprolites. Many of the nutrients survive to tell their story and, if archaeologists are really lucky, they may even find some fossilized, undigested food.

One important distinction between our relatives on the savannah and their predecessors was that they ate meat and fish. The meat they ate was lean – typical of the wild animals they hunted – and it was packed with energy and protein. This was just what this new species needed to thrive and survive. But most of their diet still consisted of leafy vegetables, young succulent shoots, and a variety of fruits, seeds and nuts.

The diet of the first humans was high in fiber, which is known to keep cholesterol levels down. Fiber passes straight through us and often absorbs waste products and water along the way. Soluble fiber also seems to slow down the absorption of glucose in the intestine – which may be important for keeping obesity at bay.

With so much vegetable matter and lean meat, our ancestors' diet was rich in unsaturated fats, which are healthier than the saturated fats and "trans fats" common in junk food. It also supplied plenty of plant sterols – the vegetable equivalent of cholesterol – that are known to reduce our blood cholesterol level. And fresh vegetables provide a wealth of chemicals known as antioxidants that help reduce damage inside the body's cells.

Three types of fat

Unsaturated fats are generally thought to be healthier than saturated fats. They are found in many foods of vegetable origin – in particular, olives, avocado, nuts and soy. Meats generally contain more saturated than unsaturated fat.

Trans fats are mainly found in processed foods. They are produced when vegetable oils are solidified to make "hydrogenated" and "partially hydrogenated" vegetable fats. As the name suggests, this process involves pumping hydrogen gas through the oil.

Popular in fast-food preparation, hydrogenated fats are melt-in-the-mouth solid, rather than liquid like vegetable oils, so they can change the texture of processed foods. They also have an increased shelf life. Without hydrogenated fat, a typical chocolate bar, for example, would only last thirty days on the shelf instead of eighteen months. However, there is growing evidence linking the consumption of trans fats with increased risk of heart disease.

Good cholesterol, bad cholesterol

When doctors measure your blood cholesterol level, they give you two readings. One is the amount of "good" cholesterol per liter, and the other is "bad" cholesterol. When foods are said to lower blood cholesterol, it means they will lower the bad cholesterol, and often increase the good.

Strictly speaking there is only one type of cholesterol – the real difference between good and bad cholesterol is in the way it is carried around in the bloodstream. Bad cholesterol is "low-density lipoprotein," LDL; good cholesterol is "high-density lipoprotein," HDL.

Bad cholesterol can accumulate in the walls of your arteries, and this seems to be part of a process called atherosclerosis, which leads to heart disease and stroke.

Junk culture

Let's travel forward through time. Along the way, we see the beginnings of agriculture – about 12,000 years (600 generations) ago. Stop by for a moment at around 10,000 years ago, and see what these farmers are eating. Domesticated animals are less athletic than wild ones, so their meat now contains more fat. Wheat has become a staple, and starchy foods like bread make up a large proportion of the diet. People consume dairy products from their cows and goats – but they still rely heavily on fresh fruits and vegetables, and of course, the bread is whole wheat.

As we get closer to the present day, we see big changes in diet after the Industrial Revolution. Much less fresh fruit and vegetables are being consumed. Hydrogenated fats have been introduced. Factory processing of foods is becoming more commonplace – it often removes fiber or destroys some of the healthful nutrients. And as the twentieth century progresses, our love of sugary, fatty foods and their increased availability are combining to make more and more people overweight.

Nowadays, a lot of people are becoming more savvy when it comes to preparing meals from fresh foods and ensuring that we have our five-a-day fruits and vegetables. But we still love heavy foods, sweets and junk. Snacks and pre-prepared food from shops and fast-food outlets are more or less the opposite of what our ancient ancestors ate. They are usually low in fiber and unsaturated fats, and contain no plant sterols and few antioxidants. In addition, they often have added salt – a major factor in raising blood pressure.

Throughout human history, our biology has stayed pretty much the same. Our bodies are still the bodies of hunter-gatherers, honed by evolution to thrive on a diet of wild vegetables, fruit and lean meat. The modern diet doesn't seem to suit it. With 6 billion of us alive today, we humans obviously do all right with our current lifestyle. But none of us wants to suffer the discomfort and the risk of early death associated with heart disease.

What can we learn from our ancient ancestors, hunting and gathering on the African savannah 180,000 years ago?

One of the scientists studying how well suited we might be to a primitive diet is Professor David Jenkins of the Department of Nutritional Sciences at Toronto University in Canada. In 2001, he began investigating the effects of an "ape diet" on people's bad cholesterol levels.

The main ingredients of Professor Jenkins' diet were soy protein, leafy greens and nuts. The participants were divided into three groups, and all tried three diets. The first was the ape diet, the second was an ordinary vegetarian diet, but with cholesterol-reducing statin drugs, and the third was an ordinary vegetarian diet without the statins. Amazingly, the people on the ape diet experienced almost exactly the same reduction in blood cholesterol as those taking statins: around 30 percent.

The science test

We set ourselves a real challenge: to reduce people's cholesterol and blood pressure in 10 days, without giving them medicines. So we decided to try our own version of Professor Jenkins' ape diet – we called it the Evo Diet. We found nine willing volunteers and fed and housed them – in a tented enclosure in Paignton Zoo, Devon. Our volunteers were all in their thirties and forties. For most of them, cholesterol and blood pressure were higher than they should have been, and most also had some family history of heart disease.

To help us run our experiment, we brought in two nutritional scientists from King's College, London: Professor Tom Sanders and Dr. Anthony Leeds. The diet was designed by a registered dietician and nutritionist, Lynne Garton. We called it the "Evo Diet," to reflect the idea that it represents what people ate early on in human evolution. The experiment was divided into two phases.

During the first half of the experiment, the diet consisted of only raw fruit, vegetables and nuts. Each subject consumed about 5.5 kilograms (12 pounds) of food every day. This part of the diet matches what we believe the very earliest humans ate. In the second half, the volunteers were allowed small amounts of cooked fish every other day, reflecting the fact that later

in our evolutionary history people began hunting as well as gathering. Overall, the diet was very low in salt and saturated fat, and high in fiber. Of course, no alcohol was allowed in the diet.

We took blood and urine samples from all nine participants at the outset, again at the midpoint of the experiment, and at the end. From the blood samples, we measured the fat content of the blood, including a breakdown into good and bad cholesterol and other fats. We measured blood pressure daily, and compared blood pressure with the concentration of sodium and potassium in the participants' urine. That way, we could tell whether any reduction in blood pressure that we observed was due to reduced salt intake.

We also carried out the same analyses on blood and urine samples from our security guards, who continued with their normal diet – this would provide extra evidence that any change in cholesterol and blood pressure was due to the special diet. The guards, husband-and-wife team Angela and Alan Butler, made sure that the experiment was carried out properly – we know that none of our volunteers escaped and visited the local watering hole, for example.

Science test results

We fed nine people a diet of fruits, vegetables and nuts, with some fish. After just ten days, our volunteers' blood cholesterol had reduced by nearly a quarter, and their blood pressure had gone down by about 10 percent.

Average reduction in cholesterol:
23 percent

So, what was the effect, if any, of twelve days of eating like our distant ancestors? Every one of our volunteers saw their cholesterol levels fall dramatically as a result of the experiment – by an average of nearly one-quarter. Six of our nine volunteers went from having cholesterol levels that were a cause of concern to levels within the normal range. This amazing result was almost certainly due to the low saturated fat content of the diet, and the high levels of fiber and plant sterols. Fiber clings to cholesterol (in the form of "bile salts") in the digestive system, so our volunteers would have been literally defecating out cholesterol. Likewise, plant sterols are similar to cholesterol, and they compete for position inside our bodies. This reduces the amount of cholesterol present.

Blood pressure was also down significantly. This was probably due to the reduced salt content of the diet, but perhaps also in part due to the fact that no alcohol was drunk.

Although this was not designed as a weight-loss diet, all of the participants lost weight during the experiment – an average of 4.4 kilograms (10 pounds) each. Importantly, they lost an average of 5.5 centimeters (2.2 inches) from their waist measurements. The diet supplied fewer calories than the volunteers were used to, and they were almost certainly more active than normal while they were inside the enclosure. Certainly just digesting all those plants would have required a lot of energy. The weight loss probably accounts for some of the reduction in blood pressure – but our experts confirmed that it could not account for it all. The very low salt content of the diet almost certainly explains the rest.

Would our volunteers consider continuing this prehistoric lifestyle for the sake of their hearts? Well, no. But all of them told us that they would be eating more fresh fruit and vegetables, and cutting down on junk food.

Anyone who has high cholesterol and is already taking statins or some other medication or nutritional supplement should not necessarily stop what they are doing and start eating a prehistoric diet. But there are lessons for all of us in this throwback to our ancestors. Cutting down on junk food and increasing your consumption of nuts and fresh fruit and vegetables has got to be a good way to stay healthy. So next time you're at the supermarket, you now know what you should be hunting and gathering.

TOP TIPS – Eating like your ancestors

If you want to try the diet the volunteers ate, think about making the following changes to your diet:

1 Aim to eat a rainbow of fruits and vegetables. Having a variety of different colored fruits and vegetables will help you get the range of nutrients you need. Eat at least five portions a day, fresh, frozen or canned – and dried fruits count too.

All the following fruit and vegetables were included in the study. Try to choose at least one fruit or vegetable from each of the following color groups each day.

COLOR	FRUIT EXAMPLES	VEGETABLE EXAMPLES
Blue/Purple	Blueberries Plums Figs	
Green	Avocados Green apples Green grapes Kiwi fruit Green pears Honeydew melon Fresh garden peas Green cabbage Zucchini	Asparagus Green peppers Broccoli Watercress Mangetout peas Sugar snap peas
White and Brown	Bananas Dates	Cauliflower Onions Mushrooms
Orange/Yellow	Apricots Satsumas Mangoes Pawpaw	Carrots Yellow peppers
Red	Strawberries Raspberries Tomatoes Cherries	Red peppers Radishes

2 Reduce your intake of saturated fat: cut down on fatty meat, meat products such as sausages, hard cheese and full-fat dairy products. Replace with oily fish, lean meats and unsalted nuts and moderate amounts of low-fat dairy products

3 Choose oils rich in monounsaturated fats such as olive oil and rapeseed oil.

4 Choose unrefined carbohydrates such as whole wheat breads and pasta, brown rice and whole grain breakfast cereals

5 Watch your salt intake: avoid adding salt to cooking and at the table, choose herbs, lemon juice and garlic for flavoring and avoid heavily salted food such as bacon, cheese, chips and smoked fish.

Three food groups essential to any Evo-Diet shopping list include:

1 Fruit and vegetables (see table)

2 Nuts
Unsalted cashew nuts
Peanuts
Walnuts
Hazelnuts

3 Fish
Fresh mackerel
Fresh trout
Fresh Dover sole

These tips were adapted from advice given by Lynne Garton, the dietician we worked with on the program.

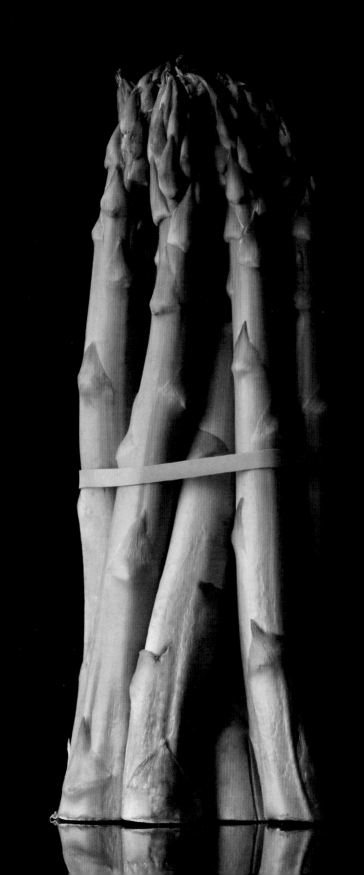

Gut flora:
cultivating your colon

When you have a throat infection, your doctor may well prescribe a course of antibiotics. These medicines kill disease-causing bacteria lurking in your body, but did you know that they could also kill off beneficial bacteria living inside you. These bacteria do an important job, helping to keep you healthy.

A good way to ensure you have enough of these beneficial bacteria is to eat "probiotics" – foods that actually contain cultures of these bacteria. But is this really such a good idea? To find out, we called in a specialist. She worked very closely with a group of modern-day cowboys – hunting for signs of bacterial life in their feces.

Good bacteria, bad bacteria

There are about 100 million million bacteria in your gut, adding just over 2.2 pounds to your body mass. Nearly all of our intestinal bacteria are found in the colon, the longest section of the large intestine. Collectively, they are called "gut flora." Each bacterium is a single cell – a tiny living thing – and a few hundred different species are present.

However, only around forty species account for the majority of the bacteria in your gut flora, and most of them are very beneficial. Others can be harmful – they cause disease. It is your mission to keep the "good" bacteria healthy and happy – and to make sure they outnumber the "bad" ones.

Before birth, the colon has no bacteria in it at all. If a baby is born vaginally, he or she will receive their first gut flora from the mother – from good bacteria hanging around down there. Research shows that babies delivered by Caesarean section have fewer beneficial bacteria, and more potentially harmful ones.

Further close contact with the mother is important. Breastfed babies also benefit: they can take in good bacteria through mouth-to-nipple contact, and the milk is perfect for feeding the gut flora. You almost certainly have the direct descendants of your mother's bacteria living inside you now.

The good bacteria are ideally suited to the environment of your colon. So they normally thrive and put severe pressure on the population of bad ones. They win the competition for space and food, so the bad bacteria are not normally able to gain a foothold. However, you unwittingly take in potentially harmful bacteria with your food, or when you put other things in your mouth. So the good bacteria must always be on their guard.

We have evolved a complex and mutually beneficial relationship with the good bacteria – a form of symbiosis that biologists call mutualism. Our side of the bargain is straightforward: we provide them with an ideal environment in which to live, and we feed them. The great thing is that we only feed them our leftovers – stuff we can't use.

The good bacteria survive by fermenting dietary fiber, found in foods of plant origin. This is one reason why you need to eat your fruits and vegetables. Your body can't digest fiber, so it passes all the way through to the colon, where the hungry bacteria are waiting.

There are two types of fiber: soluble fiber, which absorbs water, and insoluble fiber, which does not. Nuts and seeds provide lots of soluble fiber, as do peas, beans and lentils. Insoluble fiber is found in rice, carrots and cucumbers. As you might expect, soluble fiber ferments more easily than insoluble fiber.

Fermenting fiber produces chemicals that can pass through the wall of your colon. And you can make use of these chemicals. In fact, about 10 percent of your energy supply comes from them.

The fermentation inside your colon helps you to absorb minerals, and some fermentation products can help fight cancer. The good bacteria fulfill several other important roles. For example, they train our immune systems when we are babies. Good bacteria also consume some of the gases produced by bad bacteria, reducing the amount you have to "expel."

Science fact: flatulence

Many of the bacteria in the gut produce gases that contribute to flatulence. Most of the gassy mixture expelled through our backsides, however, is simply air that we have swallowed.

Gut flora: the good guys

The most important good bacteria are from the families *Lactobacillus* and *Bifidobacterium*. Both families can help prevent the formation of cancerous tumors.

***Lactobacillus* bacteria produce lactic acid, which seriously dents the population of bad bacteria. They can also produce vitamins K and B12, which we absorb through the colon wall. *Bifidobacterium* bacteria make up 90 percent of a breastfed baby's gut flora. A study published by the Allergy Research Centre in Stockholm in 2001 followed newborns through to two years old, and found that the ones who had more gut flora bacteria had less chance of developing allergies.**

Gut reaction

Most of the time, the good bacteria thrive and are in control of things down there. But if you are

Gut flora: the bad guys

Among the bad bacteria that are our colon's normal inhabitants are the family *Bacteroides*. To be fair, they do ferment carbohydrates and help to ward off even worse bacteria. But they are to blame for around 70 percent of all internal infections. Once they get out of your colon and into other parts of your body, you had better watch out. *Bacteroides* are very common in your gut – there are about 100,000 million of them in every gram of your feces.

The family of gut bacteria with the worst reputation is *Escherichia coli*. Members of this family are naturally present in large numbers in your gut. Again, they are usually classed among the good guys. And like *Bacteroides*, most *E. coli* bacteria only cause disease if they get out of your gut. For example, they will give you cystitis if they get into the urinary tract and peritonitis if the wall of the colon is punctured.

The outsiders

The worst bacteria of all are the ones that are not normally meant to be there. Many different species can form successful colonies under certain circumstances. Among the most harmful ones are from the species *Clostridium difficile*. Unfortunately, these bacteria are resistant to most antibiotics, and to acid. So they can make it through the acidic stomach and into the intestine.

Infections of *C. difficile* are very common in hospitals. After a course of antibiotics, while the normal gut flora is in decline, they thrive. And when their numbers increase, they can cause inflammation of the colon (colitis), and the toxins they produce give you diarrhea.

ill, stressed, very tired, or taking antibiotics, your gut flora suffers.

When your gut flora is in decline, the harmful bacteria can grow into a formidable force, and of course the good bacteria are no longer able to do their important jobs. When too little fiber ferments in your gut, your feces can retain too much liquid, resulting in "watery stools." With an underpopulated gut flora, you will also probably have very irregular bowel movements, you will feel lethargic, and you may notice that you fart more than normal.

So you're convinced that you need to keep your good bacteria happy and healthy. The question is how? Eating more fiber is the obvious answer – having a high-fiber diet can ensure that your gut flora stays strong. Then, of course, there are products that you can buy. Some companies produce foods or supplements with the aim of repopulating your colon. There are two types: probiotics and prebiotics.

Probiotics have been available in health food shops and supermarkets for many years. They contain living cultures of good bacteria, most often *Lactobacillus* or *Bifidobacterium* species. They are available in milk-based drinks, yogurts and cheeses. The lactic acid that the bacteria produce is responsible for the sour taste of probiotic products.

The idea behind probiotics is that they introduce colonies of good bacteria into the colon. Eating probiotic products is like infecting yourself in a good way. Some research suggests that only a small proportion of the bacteria in probiotics make it through to the colon – many are killed in the acidic conditions in the stomach.

Science fact: acidophilus

After prescribing antibiotics, some doctors also prescribe a probiotic product that contains *Lactobacillus acidophilus* – commonly known simply as *acidophilus*.

Even if they make it to the colon, the good bacteria in probiotic products may only form temporary colonies. This may be enough to allow the existing colonies to regain their numbers, but only if the conditions that led to the decline of the normal gut flora have changed.

Prebiotics, on the other hand, do not contain any live bacteria. Instead, they are food for the good bacteria. It's a bit like using fertilizer on an unhealthy lawn. Prebiotics are indigestible carbohydrates that encourage the existing good bacteria to thrive. Basically, they are soluble fiber, and good sources include Jerusalem artichokes, onions, garlic and bananas.

You can buy products that have had prebiotics added to them. They can be supplements in almost any type of food – not just milk-based products – and the fact that they contain no live bacteria means that they can have a long shelf life. Most nutritionists argue that you need to eat huge amounts of prebiotic substances to make any real difference to the good bacteria living in your gut, while others suggest that they are just as effective as probiotics.

Are probiotics and prebiotics really successful in restoring the health of your gut flora? And which are best? To find out, we carried out our own experiment on the world inside the colon.

The science test

So, which are most helpful for your beneficial bacteria: probiotics or prebiotics? We carried out our test at a ranch in Colorado. We managed to round up twelve volunteers, all of whom were staff working on the ranch. Just like traditional cowboys, our volunteers normally eat a lot of gassy beans and protein-rich red meat. Both of these foods have an effect on gut flora, so our results would be interesting.

To help us with our week-long experiment, we enlisted an expert that we playfully referred-to as "Miss Poo." Actually, her name is Gemma Walton, a researcher at the School of Food Biosciences at the University of Reading.

At the beginning of the week, Gemma took feces samples from all the participants. Then we randomly split our twelve volunteers into three groups: Group One drank a probiotic yogurt drink every day, in addition to their normal diets. Group Two consumed prebiotics in a concentrated form, as an added ingredient in orange juice. Group Three ate a diet rich in foods that have a high concentration of prebiotics. They ate chicory root, onions, garlic, artichoke and banana. At the end of the week, Gemma collected another set of samples from our volunteers.

All the samples were flown to Reading, where Gemma compared the various samples, estimating populations of good and bad bacteria. To do this, she used a technique called fluorescent in-situ hybridization (FISH). She added specially chosen molecules called "probes," which attach to the bacteria's DNA. These molecules glow, or fluoresce, under ultraviolet light. The probes she used highlighted the good bacteria, and it was possible to work out how many of these were present in each stool.

Science test results

To find out if diet could affect the populations of bacteria in the large intestine, we fed three groups three different week-long diets. One group had probiotics (containing good bacteria), one group had prebiotic foods (naturally high in fiber), and the third group drank orange juice fortified with prebiotic foods.

The fortified orange juice was the most successful. The red dots in these photographs show good bacteria in the feces of one of those volunteers, before and after the experiment.

In our experiment, the most effective way to make the good intestinal bacteria thrive was to take the orange juice drink with added prebiotics. The naturally prebiotic foods also had a positive effect on the population of good bacteria, although further analysis revealed that they also encouraged the growth of not-so-good *Clostridium* bacteria. Gemma suggested that these bacteria had probably arrived in something the volunteers ate, but it appears that they benefited from the prebiotics.

The probiotic yogurt produced no noticeable effect: this is probably because the number of bacteria present in the yogurt is so small compared to the population already in the gut. Previous studies have shown that probiotic foods can make a difference in certain circumstances. If, for example, the population of good bacteria is low – if you've had a course of antibiotics, or if you are elderly, for example – then a regular intake of probiotic products can be beneficial. And some experts in gut flora suggest that regular doses of probiotics can be beneficial to everyone.

TOP TIPS – Gut flora

To maintain the positive effects on your gut flora, you need to take probiotics and prebiotics regularly, preferably once a day in the morning.

Certain groups of the population, who might be more vulnerable to stomach upsets, such as the elderly, young children and frequent travelers might benefit from taking prebiotic- and probiotic-enriched foods.

Dietary fiber:
just passing through

You put food in at one end of your digestive system and whatever your body doesn't need emerges at the other end. That is the way many people think about digestion. And when it comes to the later stages of the journey – the colon and the rectum – many of us would rather not think about it at all.

But there's danger down below, and getting the inside story on your large intestine might just save your life. Of all cancers, colon cancer is the second biggest killer worldwide. But if treated in time, patients have a good chance of recovery. And understanding your diet might help prevent it in the first place.

Some medical research suggests that a diet rich in fiber may help to reduce your risk of getting this disease. Frustratingly, other research suggests not. We thought we'd better get the inside story on dietary fiber and what it does inside our bowels.

For our investigation we found two truckers whose intake of fiber was well below the recommended amount. We followed them while they headed south through Europe, taking lots of photographs along the way. At the end of their long-haul road trip we went on another journey – southward through their digestive systems.

Roughing it

In our parents' day it was called roughage. It has no nutritional value and eating it means you have to empty your bowels more often. Dietary fiber is one of those things that might make you think "why bother." But fiber plays a vital role in digestion. It is basically any carbohydrate you can't digest. All of it comes from plants, and there are two types: soluble and insoluble.

Good sources of soluble fiber are oats, nuts, peas and beans, and soft fruits such as apples and blueberries. Good sources of insoluble fiber are whole grain foods, couscous, carrots, cucumber and bran. Most fruits and vegetables actually contain both types. To understand the difference between soluble and insoluble fiber, let's follow their progress through your digestive system.

You're in from work and you want an easy-to-make supper. So you switch on the oven and pop in a potato. An hour or so later, you heat some baked beans on the range. Hey presto, a fiber-rich meal with the minimum of fuss. The potato skin contains about 5 grams of insoluble fiber, and the serving of baked beans provides about 10 grams of soluble fiber.

Cut a piece of baked potato, scoop up some beans with it, and put the whole lot in your mouth. Immediately, enzymes in your saliva begin to break down most of the carbohydrates in the food, turning them into glucose. But those enzymes can't touch the fiber. Once the mashed-up food reaches your stomach, different enzymes start to break down the proteins. The stomach mashes up the food even more. Again, the fiber survives unscathed.

After it leaves your stomach, the food is pushed into your small intestine. Bile is added, which will help to break down any fats – how much butter did you put on that potato? As the mixture moves through your small intestine, the nutrients break down even more. Then the broken-down carbohydrates and proteins pass into your bloodstream, and the broken-down fats pass into your lymphatic system and go straight to your liver before passing into your blood.

But still the fiber hasn't broken down.

Slowing down, speeding up

Soluble fiber absorbs water and bloats up inside you to form a thick gel. The thickened mixture of fiber and undigested food moves slowly through your small intestine. As well as thickening the whole mixture, the soluble fiber holds on to some of the nutrients, which means those nutrients are absorbed more gradually.

The slow absorption of glucose thanks to soluble fiber in the intestines is great for everyone. Research shows that this slow release reduces the likelihood of obesity and adult-onset diabetes.

The thickened soluble fiber also holds onto cholesterol from the bile. This means less cholesterol is reabsorbed. So eating soluble fiber can reduce your blood cholesterol level. By the time the mixture enters your large intestine, all the nutrients have been absorbed. What is left behind is mostly bile and fiber.

Science fact

Dietary fiber is any carbohydrate your body can't digest. It can help to keep you regular.

The main part of your large intestine is the colon, which is more than 150 centimeters (about five feet) long. Its main purpose is to absorb water back into the body. But the soluble fiber in the mixture inside your colon still holds on to some of the water. This is a good thing, because it means that your feces – or stools, as doctors like to call them – will not be too dry and hard. People who do not eat enough fiber risk becoming constipated.

Inside your colon, the soluble fiber provides food for billions of friendly bacteria. In other words, foods high in soluble fiber are "prebiotic." Without fiber to feed on, these beneficial organisms would not thrive as they do.

Unlike soluble fiber, insoluble fiber doesn't make a gel with water, and it won't even ferment. It just moves through your system unchanged, taking up space. This can reduce your appetite, which is great if you're on a diet because insoluble fiber contains no available calories. It also bulks out your stools. This keeps your colon open, preventing it from going into spasm. So fiber makes irritable bowel syndrome less likely.

By bulking up your stools, fiber also makes you produce feces more often – which, believe it or not, is almost certainly a benefit. To see why, we need to enter into the strange world of enemas, and the heated debate about colon cancer.

Toxic waste

In case you've ever wondered, a healthy stool is about 70 percent water. Up to two-thirds of its dry weight consists of bacteria from the gut. Then there is bile and, of course, fiber – all coated in a layer of mucus from the lining of your colon. There are also some substances that are toxic. They include chemicals produced by certain gut bacteria, but also some compounds from food that could not be absorbed on the long journey through your digestive system.

In the nineteenth century, many people believed that toxins were absorbed into the body from stools while they were in the colon. These toxins were blamed for many, if not most, diseases. More toxins would be absorbed if stools hung around for longer, which was supposed to explain why people feel nauseous when they are constipated. Some alternative health practitioners still promote this idea. No wonder enemas are so popular.

A fiber-rich diet keeps you regular – constipation is almost unheard-of in people who eat lots of fruit and vegetables. And so, in the 1930s, medical researchers began suggesting that a diet high in fiber might help to prevent diseases of the colon.

In the 1960s, an Irish doctor named Denis Burkitt came up with a revolutionary theory. He was working in Uganda where people ate lots of fiber and had healthy and regular bowel movements, and where very few people suffered from colon cancer. In the West, colon cancer was on the increase, and diets were very much lower in fiber.

Burkitt suggested that certain substances in food were causing the cancer. In Uganda, where high-fiber diets meant that nothing hung around for long in the colon, this would not be a big problem. But in the low-fiber diets of the West, the cancer-causing substances (carcinogens) would hang around for longer, accounting for the higher rates of the disease. Also, because soluble fiber holds on to water in the colon, it would dilute the carcinogenic substances, making them less potent. Again, this would apply less to people in the low-fiber West.

Since Dr. Burkitt's study, scientists have discovered several possible candidates for the carcinogenic chemicals. Some compounds in bile, for example, are known to be slightly carcinogenic. And there are carcinogenic compounds in burnt meat and fish. In laboratories, these compounds have caused colon cancer when fed to rats. And those same chemicals have been found in human colons. However, if you think that means Denis Burkitt's ideas must be universally accepted by now, you'll need to think again.

Trouble down below

Colon cancer is also called colorectal cancer, or bowel cancer. It starts when cells in the lining of the colon multiply too quickly, and fail to die off. This forms a polyp, which can then go on to become a cancerous tumor. The tumor can block the passage of stools, or cause blood to appear

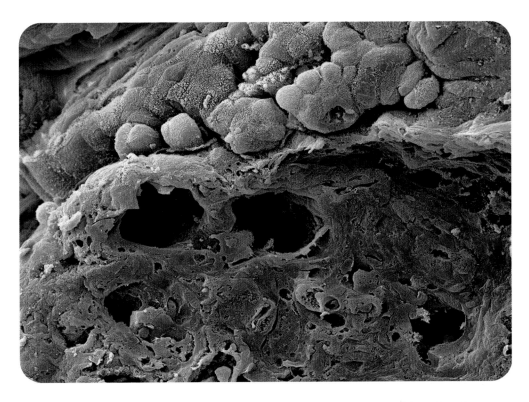

Colon cancer is caused by the rapid growth of cells, normally on the lining of the colon. Here, cancer cells are colored pink. They are growing into a tumor, which is spreading downward through the colon wall (colored brown).

in your feces. But it's most dangerous when it spreads to other parts of the body.

Every year, nearly a million new cases of colon cancer are identified worldwide. In the UK, the disease claims 16,000 lives each year – in the USA, around 50,000. Screening of the over-fifties could improve the survival rate of the disease by 80 percent. Of course, scientists are still working hard to discover just what causes the disease. And there's a bit of a controversy over what part fiber might play in helping prevent it.

The results of a huge, Europe-wide investigation into the link between diet and colon cancer was published in 2005. It was part of the even bigger study called the European Prospective Investigation into Cancer and Nutrition (EPIC). The survey's findings supported the idea that dietary fiber can reduce a person's chances of developing colon cancer. It examined the eating habits of more than 500,000 people. According to the results, people who eat the most fiber – 35 grams per day – have a 40 percent lower risk of developing colon cancer than people who take in about 10 grams per day.

But later that same year, the *Journal of the American Medical Association* published a study that had a very different finding. This research combined the results of several individual studies, effectively analyzing the diets of more than 800,000 people. It found no link whatsoever. This situation is typical of the scientific studies into colon cancer: about half of them seem to say fiber makes a difference, the rest say no.

If fiber can help to prevent colon cancer, it might not work in the way Dr. Burkitt suggested. Many different processes can start cancer – maybe fiber somehow slows down or prevents them? It is possible that a chemical called butyrate is involved. This is known to have anti-cancer properties and it is produced when soluble fiber ferments in the colon.

Of course, any cancer-fighting effects associated with eating a high-fiber diet might have nothing to do with fiber but more to do with fruits and vegetables in general. Fruits and vegetables are high in antioxidants, for example – compounds known to reduce various health risks, including cancers.

Science fact

Despite the health benefits of dietary fiber, most people eat much less than they should. Recommendations of how much fiber you should eat vary from 18 to 25 grams per day, but average consumption in the UK is just 12 grams per day.

The science test

We were frustrated by the unresolved debate over fiber and colon cancer. There was no way we could rival huge scientific studies involving half a million people or more. But we could at least test the idea that fiber speeds up the transit time of food through your guts, and keeps you regular. Helping us was Dr. Mark McAlindon, Consultant Gastroenterologist, Royal Hallamshire Hospital, Sheffield.

We went in search of truckers whose intake of fiber was low, so we could find out whether adding fiber to their diet would make things move a bit faster. We weren't disappointed. Our two volunteers, Don and Wolfgang, loved red meat, French fries, cake, chips and white bread; they had little time for fresh fruits and vegetables.

Our first task was to find out how long food normally takes to get from one end of each trucker's digestive system to the other. So as they set out together on a journey through Europe, they swallowed a small pill called a Patency Capsule, and we started the stopwatch. We could track the progress of the capsule through the truckers' bodies using a hand-held scanner. We passed the scanner over every time the truckers went to the toilet, and when finally the capsule was no longer present, we stopped the clock.

Following food

We wanted to find out whether a high-fiber diet could reduce the journey time through the digestive system – could fiber really keep you regular? We found two volunteers, who abandoned their normally low-fiber diets for ten days, eating bran flakes, whole wheat bread and lots of fruits and vegetables, instead of fast food, white bread and cake.

Each of our volunteers swallowed a special capsule with an electronic tag, which meant we could follow it as it moved through the digestive system with the slowly digesting food.

After this first measurement, we asked nutritionist and dietician Lynne Garton to come up with a high-fiber diet plan for each driver, based on each one's normal eating habits. The drivers began following their new diets, and after ten days we measured the "transit time" again.

We knew that soluble fiber might actually slow the food mixture in the small intestine, because it makes a thick gel. But in the large intestine, the colon, the bulking effect of fiber should speed things up considerably. Overall, we expected the total time from mouth to toilet to reduce considerably on the high-fiber diet. As you can see from the table, we were not disappointed.

So, eating more fiber does make you more regular, and reduces the journey time through your digestive system. Whether that reduces the risk of colon cancer is still not certain. But most scientists agree that dietary fiber is beneficial in other ways. It can help to reduce the incidence of heart disease, inflammatory bowel disease, hemorrhoids, irritable bowel syndrome, constipation, diabetes, obesity...

Science test results

Our two volunteers, Don and Wolfgang, normally eat very little fiber. For our experiment, they ate high-fiber diets for ten days. As expected, this made a huge difference to the "transit times," from mouth to toilet, through their digestive systems.

Before (low-fiber diet)

❉ Don – 22 hours and 39 minutes

❉ Wolfgang – 42 hours and 25 minutes

After (high-fiber diet)

❉ Don – 10 hours and 58 minutes

❉ Wolfgang – 12 hours and 30 minutes

Making sure you have more fiber in your diet really can keep things moving.

TOP TIPS – Getting your fiber

Aim for at least 18g of fiber a day. Here are some examples of the fiber content of foods in a typical serving size.

Food/portion size	Fiber content (grams)
Whole wheat spaghetti (3–4 tablespoons = 150g)	5
Shredded wheat (2 biscuits = 44g)	4.4
Bran flakes (4 tablespoons = 30g)	4
Whole wheat bread (2 average slices)	4
Parsnips (3 tablespoons =80g)	3.8
Peas (3 tablespoons =80g)	3.8
Lentils, green (2 tablespoons = 80g)	3
Blackberries (2 heaped tablespoons = 80g)	2.5
Dried apricots (4 apricots = 30g)	2
Muesli (3 tablespoons = 30g)	2
Porridge (4 tablespoons = 100g)	1

TRUTH ABOUT FOOD NO. 1:

YOU CAN REDUCE CHOLESTEROL AND BLOOD PRESSURE WITHOUT USING DRUGS.

THE TRUTH ABOUT FOOD

TRUTH ABOUT FOOD NO. 2:

BROCCOLI'S SUPER-CHEMICAL, SULFORAPHANE, FIGHTS CANCER.

Detox:
time for a clear-out

It's Monday morning. The excessive wine consumption that seemed such a good idea on Saturday night has finally caught up with you. A sociable, long weekend has passed – another stream of late nights, rich food, raucous laughter and general self-indulgence. The daily routine was thrown out the window, along with your sense of reason. Sound familiar?

Add everyday stress and pollution to the equation and you're probably feeling exhausted, and your body is screaming out for a thorough spring clean. Time to clear out, refresh, reenergize: time for a "detox."

Detoxing is a popular cure-all. There are detox clinics, detox holidays, detox starvation diets. There are hundreds of detox products available: facemasks, shampoos and body wraps; foot spas, digestive cleansers and "chelation therapies"; homeopathic and herbal detox remedies. And of course, there are books explaining how to choose from all of the above.

But does any of this paraphernalia actually work? We wanted to find out, so we dragged a team of volunteers from a muddy field after a rock festival. With the music still ringing in their ears – and dizzy with too much beer and wine and not enough sleep – our exhausted helpers were more than willing to give detox a go.

Pills, potions and starvation

There are two main approaches to detoxing. You can starve your body, the idea being that it will cleanse itself from the inside, or you can actively remove toxins using potions and pills. Many detox products and programs combine the two.

The classic detox is a full-on fast. By not eating for a few days, you supposedly stop the constant abuse your body normally has to deal with. This gives it a chance to clear itself of toxins – to put its house in order, to rebalance. You may feel nauseous, but that's just because all those toxins are being released into your bloodstream. Detox advocates claim that water is an essential part of the process: it helps to flush away the toxins, they say, so that you can urinate them out.

A less extreme version of the detox fast is a detox diet. Just cut out everything except small portions of fresh fruit and vegetables, and in some cases live, natural yogurt. Of course, those fruits and vegetables must be organically grown – otherwise you'll just be loading up on pesticides – won't you?

Organic versus non-organic food

Many people choose organic food because they believe it is better for their health. Foods labeled as "organic produce" have been grown without using artificial fertilizers, pesticides and antibiotics.

However, there is no convincing evidence that non-organic foods are harmful to health. The human body is capable of dealing with both "natural" and "synthetic" compounds in the tiny amounts present in our food. There is also no evidence that organic produce is more nutritious or that it tastes better than non-organic produce.

Choosing organic may not make a difference to your health, but it can still be a wise choice – for the environment. Organic farming is generally more energy-efficient and produces less waste than non-organic farming. And the chemicals used in non-organic farming can harm wildlife and affect the quality of the soil.

Who needs enemas?

Many detox starvation diets also focus on the health of your colon. Fans of colon detoxing claim that each of us carries around several pounds of gluey, hardened mucus and feces on the lining of the colon. No wonder they advocate regular enemas. Some people suggest adding essential oils, or even coffee, to the warm water used in the enema.

Medical professionals use enemas to treat a specific range of symptoms. But most would suggest that there is no benefit to be had from regular colon cleansing. And the risks – of infection, of disturbing the population of colon bacteria, and of perforation of the bowel, for example – almost certainly outweigh the benefits, especially if it's a do-it-yourself job. By the way, surgeons who have looked inside countless colons have never found congealed mucus and hardened feces. Perhaps there's no need for that enema after all.

Alongside detox diets, which allow toxins to come out of their own accord, there are thousands of products and procedures that promise to drag toxins kicking and screaming from your body.

Another approach is to try drawing out toxins through the skin. A hot bath – perhaps with added ginger or garlic – makes you sweat profusely, and is supposed to release toxins from your overloaded body, through your pores.

Detox footpads are very popular at the moment. They are cotton pads that you wear while you sleep and which contain mysterious, exotic substances that attract the toxins. By the morning, the pad has turned black. Some manufacturers claim that the dark residue is made of toxins drawn out through your feet; others simply say that the product turns black if it is "doing its job."

You can also buy a detox foot spa: add a little salt to the water and pass a gentle electric current through. This attracts the toxins and, hey presto, after half an hour the water has turned muddy brown. Of course, the brown color could be rust from the iron electrodes: exactly the same happens when you don't have your feet in the spa.

Or you might want to try an oral chelation kit, which is designed to draw out metals from fatty tissues so that you can urinate them out. Its supporters also claim that it removes calcium from "hardened" deposits in your arteries – believed to be the main cause of heart disease.

Doctors do prescribe chelation drugs to patients with serious diseases that load their bodies with too much iron, and to the tiny number of people who are exposed to high levels of heavy metals. But there is no evidence whatsoever that most people need chelation therapy, or that it reduces the risk of heart disease.

A less well-known detox treatment is the liver flush. Many thousands of people carry out this strange procedure once a month. There are several different recipes, but most of them involve drinking large amounts of olive oil mixed with fruit juice and Epsom salts. Fast for a day or so, then take the mixture at regular intervals.

Amazingly, semi-solid "stones" emerge, which fans of the treatment say are liver stones and gallstones. A net slung underneath the toilet seat catches the "stones" that emerge in your diarrhea, but skeptics suggest that these are really a soap-like substance created by the action of enzymes on the olive oil and Epsom salts.

Despite their popularity, many of these bizarre detox products almost certainly clean out nothing more than your bank account. But detoxing has become so ingrained in our culture that you can go on courses to detox your mind, and even detox your relationship.

Breaking it down

Just what are the toxins we are so desperate to shed? Not the chemicals found in coffee, tea, alcohol and junk food – the body has very efficient ways of dealing with these things. Not even nicotine, cannabis or ecstasy hangs around. They have an effect, but they are swiftly despatched by chemical reactions in the liver. After all, why would the body want to hang on to them?

While they are in your body, toxic substances can do plenty of harm. A drug overdose or a venomous snake bite can be fatal, for example. And if you have ever woken up saying "never again" after drinking a little too much the night before, then you will know what effect toxins can have.

We process alcohol into a mildly toxic chemical called acetaldehyde, which causes some of the symptoms of a hangover. And along the way, another chemical is produced that slows down the release of glucose from the liver. This results in low blood sugar, which makes you feel dizzy and lethargic, and less able to concentrate. It's no wonder people ask "what's your poison?"

But the point is that the body shows toxins the door. The tiny amounts of toxic substances that your body does store – in fat cells – are safely locked away and do you no harm. They can be released when your body starts to burn fat, but unless you lose weight dangerously quickly they never reach harmful concentrations.

So why do we feel nauseous after a few days of fasting, if it's not the effect of stored toxins leaching out? First and unsurprisingly, it could be simple lack of food. Second, if your body is used to certain chemicals such as caffeine, you can experience withdrawal symptoms if you don't have them. A few days later the symptoms go away and you may even feel better than ever.

People often report this after a gentle detox diet. Who wouldn't feel better after cutting out coffee and cigarettes, eating fresh fruit and vegetables, relaxing more, and going to bed early? And simply doing something for yourself can make you feel good. Perhaps you should see it as a new approach to healthy living, not a temporary solution that rids you of accumulated toxins, allowing you to "retox" all over again.

We put our dazed and confused volunteers through two different detox plans. Did they feel any better?

Science fact

Anything can be toxic in sufficient quantities – even water can poison you if you have too much. When dealing with toxins, "dose" is very important.

The science test

The British summer is never quite wet enough to stop hardy festival-goers enjoying a long weekend in the mud listening to their favorite bands and overdoing it a bit. What better test of a detox diet than a group of weary, wasted young women, just back from their prime position in front of the main stage at a pop festival?

We took ten volunteers from the festival, and put them on to a specially-designed detox regime. We whisked them away to country cottages in Devon. Five of them acted as "experimental controls." They followed a "normal" healthy diet. All the women were between the ages of nineteen and thirty-three.

At the outset, and again at the end, we ran tests on all ten of our volunteers, to find out their "toxic load," and to assess how well their bodies' own detox systems were working. Emily Russell, research nurse at the Hammersmith Hospital, carried out the tests for us.

The detox experiment

We asked three experts to pull together some general principles typical of published detox regimes.

1   No processed food. Nothing from a packet and nothing you haven't made yourself.
2   No added salt.
3   No added sugar.
4   No tea or coffee (not even decaffeinated).
5   No wheat.
6   No red meat.
7   No dairy produce.
8   No booze.
9   No concentrated drinks; definitely no soft drinks.
10 Organic produce wherever possible.

Our experts were dieticians Nigel Denby (Queen Charlotte's and Hammersmith Hospitals), Jacqui Lowton (Children's Hospital for Wales), and private clinical nutritionist Peter Cox. Nigel Denby made the final decision about what the detox girls should eat.

Helping us to plan and carry out the experiment were two experts in toxicology from Imperial College, London: Professor Alan Boobis, OBE and Professor Martin Wilkins. Nutritionist Professor Gary Frost, from the University of Surrey, checked over what we were feeding the "detoxers" and also the diet enjoyed by members of the control group, who did not follow the detox plan. We provided the control group with a diet based on healthy eating guidelines.

What we measured

We investigated kidney function by measuring the level of creatinine in the women's urine. Creatinine is produced by the breakdown of a chemical in your muscles; a healthy kidney allows a fairly constant amount of this substance into your urine.

We also checked the women's liver function. To do this, we fed them a controlled amount of caffeine and waited for the liver to process it. The chemicals that result from the breakdown of caffeine can be measured in saliva, and they provide a fairly reliable measure of liver function.

We then gave all the women a blood test to find the concentrations of aluminium – a metal commonly used in take-out food cartons and kitchen foil. Finally, we measured levels of key antioxidants (vitamin C and vitamin E) in the women's blood.

The results were interesting. There was no noticeable difference between the two groups: the detox diet had no effect. Livers and kidneys were functioning just as well in the non-detox group as in the detoxers. Both groups had similar concentrations of antioxidant vitamins, too. The strict "detox" regime made no difference whatsoever.

TOP TIPS – Detox diets

❈ There's no good evidence to show that starving ourselves actually rids us of the toxins we think are clogging up our bodies. We possess the ultimate detox machines already: our liver and kidneys. Most people will find that they lose weight on a detox diet simply because they have reduced their calorie intake.

❈ Avoid the quick-fix detox and instead opt for a more balanced approach. Cut the calories from high-fat, high-sugar foods and replace them with filling fruits and vegetables for that fuller feeling with fewer calories and real weight loss, rather than water loss.

❈ It does make sense to reduce the amount of detoxing the liver has to do by cutting down on alcohol and caffeine.

❈ Fluids are essential to life so make sure you stay fully hydrated.

❈ Frozen foods often contain fewer additives such as preservatives than chilled ready-meals.

Broccoli cancer protection:
are you getting it?

It's not everyone's favorite vegetable: broccoli is often found sulking in the leftover sauce at the end of Sunday lunch. Most kids find it pretty disgusting. George Bush Senior banned it from the White House when he was president. Well, who needs it? Anyone who truly hates broccoli can choose from a huge selection of other fruits and vegetables to make up their five-a-day target.

But broccoli-haters might want to try striking up a better relationship with this vegetable after all. The reason? More than any other vegetable, broccoli and its close relatives can protect against cancer. A remarkable chemical found in them can help to stop this evil disease in its tracks.

There is a complication, however. Only about half of the population can benefit fully from broccoli's amazing anti-cancer action. The rest will urinate out most of the special chemical before it can work its wonders.

Broccoli history

For many people, broccoli is a bit like the archetypal clever kid who sits in the corner – full of virtue but not very interesting. But it hasn't always been this way. Broccoli was on the A-list in Ancient Rome.

The Romans regularly served broccoli in wine, cream or herb sauces, and they even cultivated new varieties. Drusus Caesar, the son of the Roman emperor Tiberius, loved broccoli so much that he ate almost nothing else for months on end. He only stopped when his father told him to – because his urine was coming out green. Nobody knows whether he benefited from eating so much of his favorite vegetable, because he was murdered while still a young man.

Nutritionally, broccoli is a real winner. It is high in fiber and calcium, and low in fat. It is a great source of folic acid and vitamin C – both of which encourage the body to absorb iron, which broccoli also contains. In fact, one cupful of cooked broccoli supplies as much calcium as a glass of milk, 10 percent of the recommended daily intake of iron and the entire daily quota of vitamin C.

Broccoli has interesting medical potential, too. It contains the trace element chromium, which may help prevent adult-onset diabetes. But the real buzz about this vegetable at the moment is due to its potent anti-cancer properties.

Science fact

Broccoli is often described as a cruciferous vegetable, because its flowers are cross-shaped. Other cruciferous vegetables include cabbage, cauliflower, Chinese cabbage, sprouts and watercress.

Fighting the good fight

Broccoli hit the headlines in 1992. For a few years, cancer researchers at Johns Hopkins University in Baltimore, Maryland, had been following a hunch: statistics showed that people who eat a lot of fruit and vegetables usually have lower rates of cancer. So they tested a range of vegetable extracts in their laboratory, looking for particular chemicals that might be able to stop or slow down the formation of cancers.

Of all the vegetables the researchers tested, the ones that showed the greatest anti-cancer effect were broccoli and its close relatives, cauliflower, kale, Brussels sprouts and cabbage. Extracts of these vegetables were particularly good at reducing the incidence of cancerous tumors in laboratory cultures.

Several months and many pounds of broccoli later, they found the chemical that seemed to be preventing cancerous tumors from forming. It is called sulforaphane – a sulfur-containing compound that is responsible for broccoli's slightly bitter smell and taste. It comes from the same family of chemicals as those responsible for the tang of mustard and horseradish.

The researchers also discovered that young broccoli shoots just a few days old have, on average, thirty times the concentration of sulforaphane found in older plants. This makes sense when you discover that sulforaphane is broccoli's built-in pesticide, designed to repel anything that tries to eat it. Plants need the greatest protection against insect attack when they're still young and tender.

The team of scientists actually patented the cultivation technique they had used, and broccoli sprouts are now on sale in health food shops and even some supermarkets in the USA. They look like cress. Incidentally, the small stalks you can buy in the supermarket are not "broccoli sprouts" – they are just small stalks from the adult plant.

Chemical combat

Cancer researchers are very excited about sulforaphane – it has shown off its anti-cancer properties in dozens of studies in laboratories all over the world. Cancer begins when mistakes appear in our DNA, which is found in most cells and carries detailed instructions for making the proteins they need to function. These instructions are copied each time our cells divide, which is happening all the time – so there is ample opportunity for mistakes.

Cancer can occur quite naturally, at random: it is a lottery you don't want to win. The

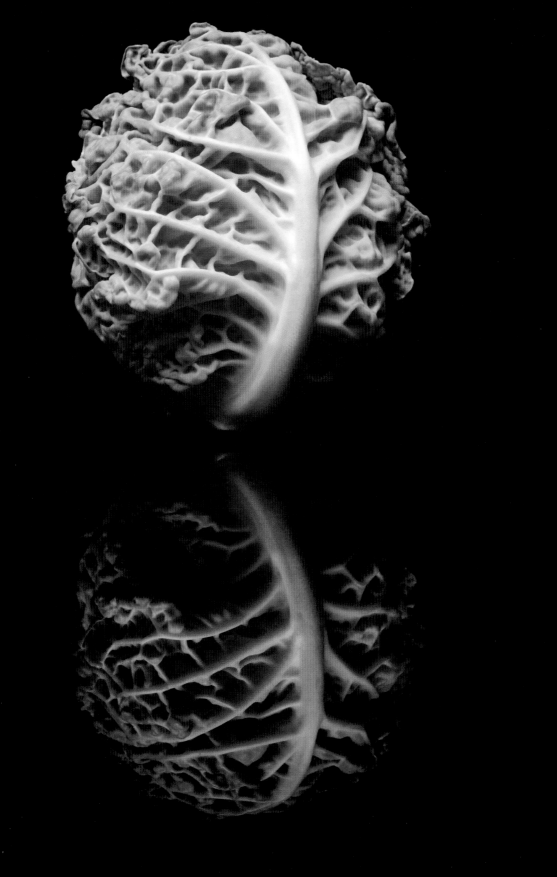

presence of certain toxic chemicals, such as those found in tobacco smoke, dramatically increases the odds. Any chemicals capable of causing cancer are called carcinogens.

Our bodies have evolved remarkable repair systems that can spot mistakes in DNA and correct them. But carcinogens make these repair systems less effective. If a mistake isn't picked up, it will be reproduced each time the DNA is copied. The most damaging types of mistake are the ones that make new cells divide uncontrollably, forming a tumor. Each new cell in the tumor carries DNA that has the mistake.

Broccoli's super-chemical, sulforaphane, fights cancer in three ways. First, it can slow everything down inside damaged cells, giving the repair systems a chance to do their work. Second, it seems to encourage cancerous cells to die off, slowing the formation of tumors.

Third, and most importantly, sulforaphane encourages our cells to produce several different enzymes that form an important line of defense in the internal battle against cancer. They are part of the body's detoxification system, and they can speed the expulsion of carcinogens.

It's in your genes

So, the meek and flowery green vegetable has more to it than you thought? Well, before you go out and buy a portion, read on. Some scientists, like Professor Richard Mithen at the Institute of Food Research in Norwich, now believe that half of us lack a specific gene that makes sulforaphane's action more potent. These same people also urinate out sulforaphane more quickly than everyone else. This means their bodies have less time to benefit from the presence of broccoli's wonder chemical.

As a result, anyone who lacks the gene

– called GSTM1 – needs to consume much more sulforaphane to get the same effect. And yes, that means more broccoli – although you could choose to eat more Brussels sprouts if you prefer.

Help is at hand for those who lack GSTM1. First, some health food shops sell young broccoli shoots, with their high sulforaphane content. Second, by combining broccoli with foods that contain the mineral selenium, you can make the effect of sulforaphane up to thirteen times as effective. Rich sources of selenium include Brazil nuts, chicken, prawns and eggs. Third, scientists at the Institute of Food Research in Norwich have bred a "super broccoli" that has more than three times the concentration of sulforaphane as ordinary varieties.

But if you want your food to help protect you against cancer, there's no need to become a modern day Drusus with a broccoli obsession. There are many other chemicals to be had that provide protection against a number of diseases, including cancer. The bottom line is that you need a balanced diet that includes a wide variety of fruits and vegetables.

DNA what you should eat?

The relationship between our genes and the food we eat is not restricted to GSTM1 and sulforaphane. For example, there is an enzyme that breaks down the pigment in beetroot. About 10 percent of people lack the gene for this enzyme, and their urine is pink after eating beetroot. A similar thing happens with asparagus – about half of us have urine that smells odd after eating it.

Pink or smelly urine is a curiosity, but having these particular genes won't make you ill. However, hundreds of genes do affect your risks of developing diseases. In many cases, eating more or less of certain foods could help us to manage those risks.

For example, we all know that too much salt is bad for us, but just how much salt we are "allowed" to eat depends upon several known genes. Some people can eat more salt and not increase their risk of high blood pressure, while the rest of us should be more careful.

The interaction between our food and our DNA is a growing area of nutritional research. A few private companies already offer a personal "DNA diet plan." You send off a scraping of cells from inside your mouth, the company analyses the DNA from the cells, looking at around twenty different genes, and creates a series of dietary recommendations just for you.

But unless you pay for such a test, there's no way of knowing whether you have GSTM1, for example. In the future, however, doctors may be able to examine your entire genome in seconds using a small device. Within minutes, they will be able to make personal recommendations about what foods you should be eating. If you are not a fan of broccoli or sprouts, chances are you will find those recommendations hard to swallow.

TOP TIPS – Wonderful broccoli

❊ There is a chemical in broccoli that helps your body fight cancer. It is not affected much by heating, but if you boil broccoli in water, some of it dissolves into the water. Steaming or microwaving it will lose less – or you could use it in a low-calorie vegetable soup.

❊ In addition to providing anti-cancer action, broccoli is a great source of fiber and vitamin C.

TOP TIPS – Binge on broccoli

❊ Other vegetables, particularly the cruciferous vegetables, contain similar compounds to broccoli, which can prevent cancer. Examples of cruciferous vegetables are kale, Brussels sprouts, cabbage, radishes and cauliflower.

SUMMARY: HOW TO BE HEALTHY

 EATING A DIET HIGH IN NUTS AND FRESH FRUIT AND VEGETABLES – SIMILAR TO WHAT OUR ANCESTORS ATE – REALLY CAN HELP CUT CHOLESTEROL AND REDUCE HIGH BLOOD PRESSURE.

 The way food interacts with your body is partly down to your genetic makeup. A chemical in broccoli, for example, seems to be very effective at fighting cancer – but only in people who have a particular version of a gene.

THERE ARE BILLIONS OF BENEFICIAL BACTERIA IN YOUR GUT. EATING FOODS HIGH IN SOLUBLE FIBER CAN HELP THEM TO HELP YOU.

It's true: eating a diet high in fiber keeps you regular. Fiber has many other health benefits, too – there is evidence that it can help prevent colon cancer, for example.

 THE BODY HAS VERY EFFICIENT WAYS OF RIDDING ITSELF OF TOXINS. THERE IS NO EVIDENCE THAT STRINGENT DETOX DIETS HAVE ANY POSITIVE EFFECTS.

2. HOW TO BE SLIM

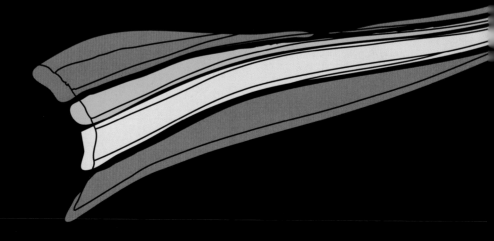

HOW TO BE SLIM

Trying to stay trim can be a real challenge – and a huge frustration. Let's face it; many of us are serial dieters. No matter how hard we try to cut back on the amount of food we eat, the pounds just keep piling on. But understanding what goes on inside your body could give you the power to control your weight.

In the UK, more than 40 percent of men and 30 percent of women are overweight, and one-quarter of all adults are "clinically obese." These figures are increasing; and although the USA has the highest rates of obesity overall, the UK has the fastest growing rate of obesity in the developed world.

We all know that being overweight poses serious risks to health – in particular, fatter people are at greater risk of heart disease, diabetes and some cancers. That's why "normal weight" is often described as "healthy weight." So why are so many of us piling on the pounds?

The basic truth is that people become overweight because they take in more energy in their food than their bodies use. The excess is stored away as fat reserves, mostly under the skin. If you are overweight, there are loads of diets to choose from. Some of them are successful for the short term; most are only as good as your willpower; lots of them don't work at all; and some can actually put your health at risk.

Ultimately the only way to lose weight is by calorie control. Take in fewer calories by managing what you eat; and use up more calories by being physically active. But, as so many of us know, that's easier said than done. And if you do manage it, the weight piles on again as soon as you stop the diet.

Keeping a lid on your calorie intake can be difficult – and it's especially important for those of us who are less active than we should be. Modern research into dieting focuses on appetite. An understanding of appetite can ensure that you take in fewer calories in your food, without feeling hungry, and without becoming malnourished.

In our investigation of obesity, we questioned a few

common myths and assumptions. Do slim people really have faster metabolisms than fatter people? Does eating more slowly make you eat less? Does a glass of water before a meal reduce your appetite? We looked at the psychology of appetite. Do bigger portion sizes make you eat more? Does the way food is presented affect how much we eat?

We also looked at some of the hot new science coming out of research labs around the world. Did you know that a diet high in calcium can help you to lose weight and keep it off? And that dairy products – often left out of dieters' shopping baskets – are the most effective source of calcium if you want to lose weight? And did you know that food high in protein can help you feel full, making you eat less?

Knowing how appetite and metabolism (energy out) work together should make it possible to control the balance between energy in and energy out. Then you can fight obesity, find a healthy weight, and say goodbye to the days of yo-yo dieting and semi-starvation.

Metabolism: burning up

You're eyeing up that second piece of cake, but you decide to leave it – you're watching your weight. Your friend, on the other hand, is enjoying what seems to be her third piece. How dare she eat as much as she likes and stay slim! She must have a much faster metabolic rate than you, you think to yourself. All those calories must get burned up rather than ending up as fat on her tummy and hips.

Think again. Thinner people actually have slower metabolisms than fatter people. Yes, you did just read what you thought you read: thinner people have slower metabolisms, not faster.

Just as a big car guzzles more gas than a small car, a larger human body burns more fuel than a smaller one. And the amount of fuel – calories – you use each day is your metabolic rate. Your thin friend has a slower metabolism than you, and is therefore burning her food more slowly than you.

If you are overweight and you want to lose the excess, it is important to understand a bit about how your metabolism works.

Busy doing nothing

If you're doing something strenuous you are clearly using lots of energy. But what you may not know is that most of your body's energy is used on just staying alive.

After a meal, the muscles of your digestive system use up energy pushing the food through you. It also takes energy to break down food. But even when you are not digesting, your body is using lots of energy. Your liver has a full-time job dealing with toxins; your brain is keeping everything in order at mission control, even while you sleep; your heart is pumping blood through your arteries and your veins. In fact, every cell in your body needs a little bit of energy just to stay alive.

The rate at which you use energy when you are doing nothing is called your basal metabolic rate. This is what most people mean when they say, "thin people have higher metabolic rates."

Go figure

Your body burns most of its calories just staying alive. Your baseline metabolic rate depends almost entirely upon your sex, your age and your body weight. Men have faster rates than women, younger people faster than older – and yes, fatter people really do have faster basal metabolic rates than slimmer people.

Going for the burn

If fatter people have higher basal metabolic rates, how come thinner people can eat so much more and still not put on weight? The truth almost always is that they don't.

Research shows that many overweight people consistently underestimate how much they eat when they fill in dietary questionnaires or keep detailed food diaries. In reality, most fat people eat more than most thin people. Strenuous exercise makes a big difference to the number of calories burnt. But so can less strenuous activities. If you spend most of your day fidgeting, you are burning up calories and making a significant addition to your overall metabolic rate. If you walk or cycle to work, wash the car by hand or simply have a job that requires you to move around a lot, you will increase your rate. The little things can make a big difference.

On the other hand, if you consistently use fewer calories than you take in, you will put on weight. It is as simple as that. You will put on one kilogram of body fat for every 7,700 kilocalories you don't use. That's one pound for every 3,500 extra kilocalories. As you gain weight, your metabolic rate increases – eventually, energy in and energy out will be in balance again.

In our high-tech, high-convenience lives we have easy access to fatty and sugary foods, which contain a ready supply of energy. And our lives are generally much less active. Is it any wonder that obesity is on the increase?

What is a calorie?

Food gives you energy. You use it to stay alive and in everything you do, but if you take in more energy than you need, your body stockpiles it as fat.

A calorie is simply a unit of energy. Look on any food product, and you will see how many calories it contains. Food energy is listed as kcal (kilocalories); one kilocalorie is equal to 1,000 calories. This can lead to some confusion.

For example, when someone says that a bar of chocolate has "250 calories," they actually mean 250 kcal.

Food energy values are also listed in kilojoules (kJ). One kilocalorie is equal to just over four kilojoules.

Calories per hour

The number of calories you burn up every hour depends very much on what you are doing. These figures are for a forty-year-old woman who weighs seventy kilograms (just over one hundred fifty-four pounds):
- ❖ **Sitting still for one hour: 90 kilocalories**
- ❖ **Walking for one hour: 280 kilocalories**
- ❖ **Jogging for one hour: 750 kilocalories**

TOP TIPS – Energy and metabolism

If you consume more calories than your daily requirement, you will put on weight. To find out your daily energy requirement:

1 Work out your basal metabolic rate (BMR)

Male	BMR = 66 + (13.7 x wt in kg) + (5 x ht in cm) – (6.8 x age in years)
Female	BMR = 655 + (9.6 x wt in kg) + (1.8 x ht in cm) – (4.7 x age in years)

To convert pounds to kilograms, divide by 2.2. To convert inches to centimeters multiply by 2.54.(This formula is the Harris Benedict Equation, and gives an accurate figure for all except the very lean and the very obese.)

2 Now multiply your BMR by the following activity factor:

		Men	Women
Inactive	Little or no exercise, desk job	1.4	1.4
Light	Some light daily exercise	1.5	1.5
Moderate	Regular aerobic exercise	1.78	1.64
Heavy	Energy-intensive job or serious athlete	2.1	1.82

Example:

Sex: Female; Weight: 70kg; Height: 167cm (5ft 6in); Age: 28; Activity level: Moderate

BMR = 655 + 672 + 300 – 131 = 1496
Energy requirement = BMR x 1.64 = 2453 .

One pound (½ kg) of body weight is equivalent to 3,500 kilocalories. To lose a pound in one week, consume 500 kilocalories less than your energy requirement every day.

Unfortunately, losing weight is not as easy as gaining it. If you put yourself on a starvation diet you will rely on fat stores, burning them to obtain energy, but your body will also start to burn up protein, causing some muscle wasting. And by cutting down your food intake, you may dramatically reduce your intake of important nutrients.

Simply exercising more may not be the answer either. The concern is that by increasing your energy demands – by doing regular strenuous activity – you will automatically take in more calories to compensate. Actually, it's not all bad news: studies suggest that this effect is more marked in slim people. So if you are overweight, your body should burn at least some of that stored fat when you exercise.

A slow and methodical approach to weight loss, with calorie control, cardiovascular and muscle-building exercise, is the best way to lose weight and keep it off. If you need to lose weight, first set yourself a realistic goal: aim for a weight loss of no more than 10 percent of your body weight. Once you've reached this goal, congratulate yourself and try to maintain this weight for a period of time before aiming for another 5 or 10 percent reduction.

And once your body is back in good shape and you have adopted a more energetic lifestyle, you will be able to match the cake intake of your friend without feeling too guilty.

Weight loss:
the calcium effect

A warm summer evening. The golden light from the setting sun makes you squint as you sip from a glass of Cabernet Sauvignon. You look down at the wedge of blue cheese left on your plate, imagine it crumbling in your fingers and melting in your mouth. But you are trying to lose weight. Hadn't you better leave it there on the plate?

Cheese is usually one of the first things to be sacrificed when people start a calorie-controlled diet. Dairy products in general have a reputation for being high in fat. Well, several pieces of recent research suggest that when you eat dairy products, not all their calories count – and it's all down to the calcium these foods contain.

Don't dump the dairy

If you are on a diet, a trip to the supermarket can be a bit of a nightmare. So much temptation. With dairy's reputation, you might be better off avoiding that aisle altogether. Dairy is versatile and packed with protein and minerals, but its downfall has always been that it is high in fat.

We all know that fat is something we need to cut down on if we are counting the calories. But imagine if some of the fat you ate could pass straight through you, so that some of the calories it contained simply didn't count. Well, if your food contains lots of calcium – as dairy produce does – then that may be exactly what happens. Add to that the fact that calcium can make your body burn off fat, and you might be heading down the dairy aisle after all.

Researchers stumbled upon the calcium weight-loss effect by accident during the 1980s while they were studying the relationship between diet and blood pressure. The effect remains controversial, but dozens of studies have added evidence that it is real, at least in people who are already overweight.

For example, in 2003, Professor Michael Zemel of the University of Tennessee carried out a study in which half the volunteers consumed three small cartons of low-fat yogurt each day as part of a calorie-controlled diet. All the volunteers consumed the same number of calories overall, but those who ate the yogurt lost 20 percent more body fat than the others, and most of that fat was lost from their bellies.

So the occasional lump of blue cheese might not be as bad for you as you think. And if you stick to low-fat dairy foods, you can welcome yogurt, cheese and milk back into your life on a regular basis. You'll probably lose more weight than you ever did without it. Keep your overall calorie intake the same, but eat more dairy and you could shed pounds.

Taking it on board

The recommended intake of calcium varies from person to person, but 1,000 milligrams (one gram) per day is a good figure to keep in mind – less for young children and more for breastfeeding mothers. A single serving of natural yogurt contains more than 400 milligrams. Exceeding one gram per day is normally OK, but it is not recommended to exceed 2,500 milligrams per day.

Other foods besides dairy produce that are good sources of dietary calcium include soft-boned fish such as salmon and sardines; beans, including baked beans; and soy milk, especially if it has been fortified with extra calcium.

Most leafy green vegetables have high calcium content. However, many of them contain oxalates: compounds that bind to the calcium, making it unavailable to the body. Vegetables that are high in oxalates include spinach, rhubarb and chard. Leafy greens low in oxalates, which are good sources of calcium, include kale, collards and mustard cress.

How does it work?

There seem to be two sides to the flab-busting effect of calcium.

First, and most surprisingly, calcium clings on to the fat inside your intestines. Together, calcium and fat form a substance very similar to soap that can't be absorbed across the wall of your intestine, so it passes out of your body.

The more calcium you have in your diet, the more fat will be excreted. And any fat that passes through you and into the toilet can't end up in fat cells under your skin. That is why in a high-calcium diet, some calories don't count.

Although the amounts of fat passed into the toilet in this way are small, they do add up. Over the course of a year on an increased calcium diet, the calories lost this way can easily be equivalent to losing 3.5 kilograms of body fat. That's a loss of more than seven pounds without reducing your calorie intake.

The second effect of dietary calcium on your body weight is more complex. Calcium plays an important role in metabolism, controlling the fat-burning machinery inside fat cells.

The human body will often slow its metabolic rate in response to a reduced-energy diet. In other words, if you reduce your calorie intake, your body may reduce the rate at which your body burns up calories, to remain in energy balance. This probably evolved to get early humans through the times when food was scarce. But nowadays it can frustrate those dieters who reduce their food energy intake but still don't lose weight.

Scientists have suggested that calcium can offset this effect, by keeping your metabolic rate normal when you are dieting. It does this by increasing the rate at which your body burns fat. What is more, calcium present in the spaces

TRUTH ABOUT FOOD NO. 3:

FATTER PEOPLE HAVE HIGHER METABOLIC RATES THAN THINNER PEOPLE, NOT THE OTHER WAY AROUND.

THE TRUTH ABOUT FOOD

TRUTH ABOUT FOOD NO. 4:
WHEN YOUR STOMACH IS EMPTY, IT PRODUCES A HORMONE CALLED GHRELIN, WHICH MAKES YOU FEEL HUNGRY.

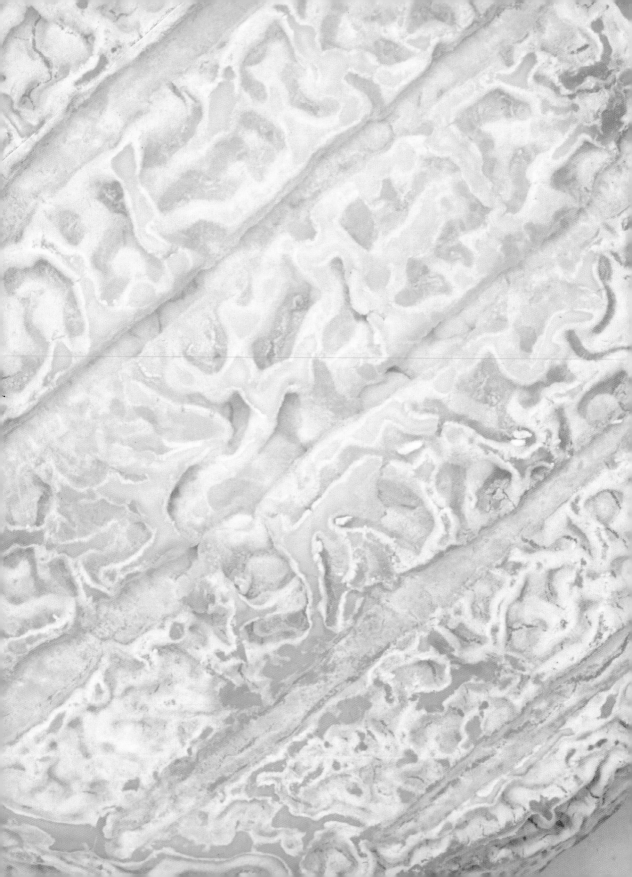

between fat cells seems to reduce the rate at which new cells form.

You can get calcium from sources other than dairy products – and any dietary calcium will do. But most studies into the calcium weight-loss effect have shown that dairy products seem to be the most effective. Researchers believe that certain chemical compounds in milk increase the amount of calcium your body absorbs. These chemicals are in the liquid part of dairy products (the whey), not the solid part (the curd).

When anything acidic such as rennet, fruit juice or vinegar is added to milk, or if it is left to stand, the solid parts gather together to form curds. This is the basis of cheese making. Soft cheeses contain some whey, but hard cheeses contain hardly any. Anything made from whole or skim milk will contain whey, and whey protein as a by-product of the cheese-making industry is added to many foods, including most breads and canned soups.

So, if there really are compounds in whey that help your body to absorb calcium, then yogurt and soft cheeses will be more effective at helping you manage your weight than hard cheeses.

The science test

We worked with Professor Arne Astrup and his team at the Royal Veterinary and Agricultural University, in Copenhagen, Denmark, to test the idea that calcium in the diet can hold onto fat. The team enlisted twelve overweight men and women. Half were put onto a low-calcium diet, which contained about half as much calcium as the average person would have. The rest were placed on a high-calcium diet, with twice the average daily intake of calcium. The diets both had exactly the same number of calories, and both had the same mix of fat, protein and carbo-

hydrates.

The diets ran for one week, and after a "wash-out" period of two weeks, the participants swapped – so that those on the low-calcium diet were now on the high-calcium diet, and vice versa. Throughout, we analyzed people's feces: we froze the feces, and measured how much fat and calcium – and how many calories – it contained.

The results were impressive. On average, the high-calcium dieters excreted 12 percent of the fat in their diet, while the low-calcium dieters excreted only 6 percent. The low-calcium dieters were excreting around 1,000 kilocalories per day in their feces. The high-calcium dieters were excreting 200 kilocalories more per day. It seems increasing your calcium intake really could help you to lose weight, and without increasing your appetite.

You're on a diet. You look at how many calories are in a cheese sandwich and you just say no. But what if not all the calories count? A few foods, like nuts, remain partially undigested when you eat them, for example, so that a small proportion of the available calories end up passing straight through you. Well, a similar thing seems to happen with foods that are high in calcium. Research has shown that calcium in foods holds on to fat, to form a substance similar to soap, which exits your system – taking fats and calories with it.

The role of calcium in weight loss is still uncertain, and the difference it makes is probably only small. But it seems that eating foods rich in calcium can help you lose weight in two ways – by making you burn more calories, and by reducing the amount of fat your body takes in. So, when you eat a cheese sandwich, the calcium in the cheese takes with it some of the fat – and the calories they carry pass straight through your body. Perhaps we don't have to count all our calories after all.

The UK Committee on the Medical Aspects of Food and Nutrition Policy set the Reference Nutrient Intake (RNI) for calcium as follows.

Age/Sex	Calcium requirement (mg/day)
Infants & children, depending on age	350–550
Teenage girls	800
Teenage boys	1,000
Adult men & women	700
Breast-feeding women	extra 550

The RNI is a daily amount that is enough or more than enough for 97 percent of people. The RNI is similar to the more familiar Recommended Daily Amount.

TOP TIPS – Calcium

Some research suggests that high-calcium diets can help to reduce weight gain. Low-fat dairy foods are a good source of calcium.

Boost your intake of **low-fat milk** (700mg calcium per quart):

✳ Splash it on breakfast cereal.

✳ Have white sauce with your main meal.

✳ Enjoy cold milk shakes and hot milky chocolate drinks.

✳ Rediscover milky puddings, such as rice puddings.

Try **low-fat yogurt:**

✳ Enjoy with breakfast cereal.

✳ Eat with chopped fresh summer fruits.

✳ Make a smoothie with your favorite fruit.

✳ Make a yogurt dressing for salads or dip in vegetable sticks as a snack.

Choose **reduced-fat cheese:**

✳ Try out the low- or reduced-fat cheeses.

✳ Make a salad with a dollop of cottage cheese, which is naturally low in calories.

Food	Serving size	Calcium content (mg)
Canned sardine with bones	1 sardine	115
Shelled prawns	2 large tablespoons (60g)	90
Baked beans	Small can (150g)	80
Sesame seeds	1 tablespoon (12g)	80
Orange	1 large	70
White or brown bread	2 large slices	70
Dried apricots	7	50
Red kidney beans	Small can (150g)	50
Cooked broccoli	2–3 tablespoons	35
Egg	1	30

Satisfaction: getting your fill

Almost every weight watcher will tell you the same story. You diet, you monitor everything you eat, and yet somehow you always fail to lose weight and keep it off. Every time we fail we blame ourselves.

But there is hope. In the past decade there have been remarkable advances in our understanding of the chemicals involved in the digestive process – and the good news is that scientists are learning about the way our appetites work. They are only at the beginning of the journey, but the more they learn the more we will understand how we can eat less.

You'll be pleased to know that the latest scientific insight might help you to feel satisfied without loading up on calories. You can take control of your desire to eat.

An appetite for dieting

Many diet plans suggest you eat less, but that can leave you feeling hungry and miserable. And if you're hungry, you are likely to break the rules of the diet – satisfying your appetite but replacing the misery with guilt.

Human appetite is complex, and science is only beginning to uncover its secrets. Doctors have long been aware that people can develop a permanent desire to eat after suffering damage to certain areas of the brain. Researchers discovered that one part of the brain, called the hypothalamus, is particularly important in regulating appetite. But they couldn't work out how the digestive system informs the brain that it has had enough.

The first important breakthrough came in 1994 with the discovery of a hormone called leptin, which is produced mostly in fat cells. Researchers were able to prove that leptin is part of a system that tells the brain to stop eating. It is produced mainly in fat cells, not the stomach or the intestines – so it is unlikely to play a role in making you stop eating at a particular sitting. Leptin controls appetite over a longer time frame.

The discovery of leptin caused a sensation, and other chemicals have been found that together form an appetite signaling chain, feeding signals from the stomach and intestines up to the brain. Most of these chemicals are produced in response to a hearty meal, and they

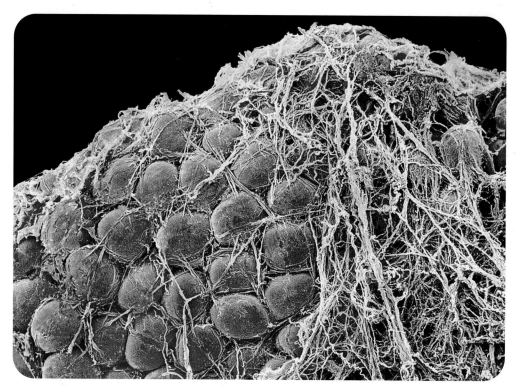

Surrounded by connective tissue, these fat cells (colored orange-red) are composed mostly of fat. They provide an insulating layer underneath the skin. Fat cells, or adipocytes, are among the largest of human cells.

circulate in the blood, finding their way to the hypothalamus, where they signal the fact that the body has had enough food for now.

One of the most important appetite messengers is ghrelin, which is produced by the stomach wall. Ghrelin is the only known appetite hormone that increases appetite. When the stomach is full, and the stomach wall is stretched, very little ghrelin is produced. But when the stomach is empty again, the stomach wall releases ghrelin into the bloodstream. When enough ghrelin reaches the hypothalamus, it makes you feel hungry. Injecting ghrelin directly into the blood makes a person feel hungry and eat more. In experiments involving people with appetite loss due to cancer, administration of ghrelin has increased the food intake by nearly a third.

Interestingly, the concentration of ghrelin in the bloodstream is higher after weight loss – a fact that may explain why it is so hard to keep the weight off once you have lost it. Knowing how leptin, ghrelin and the other appetite messengers work means we are close to understanding how to lose weight painlessly and successfully.

It is easy to see the importance of research into appetite – and it is no surprise that pharmaceutical companies are funding some of the cutting edge research. Dieting is big business, and finding a safe appetite suppressant could prove to be a bigger moneymaker than Viagra.

There are already some promising

drugs in the pipeline, and a few have even hit the market. For example, in June 2006 Britain became the first country to license Rimonabant, which is said to reduce body weight by up to 10 percent.

But not every weight watcher wants to take drugs to suppress hunger pangs. The Holy Grail is to eat great food, not feel hungry and still lose weight. Impossible? Well, maybe not. Some foods really do fill you up without filling you out.

Feeling full for longer

Controlling your appetite can be the key to weight loss. If you are hungry, strong cravings will make you give in sooner or later. If you feel full, you'll eat less and you will lose weight. It is every weight watcher's ultimate fantasy to diet without feeling hungry.

The new buzzword in dieting is "satiety." The more satiated you feel after one meal, the less food you'll eat at the next one – or the longer you'll leave it until you eat again. Fill up, but with as few calories as possible, and you will be on the way to becoming a successful dieter.

In 1995, Dr. Susanna Holt at the University of Sydney, Australia, devised a satiety index – a scale of how much different foods fill us up. Dr. Holt asked a group of students to eat exactly 240 kilocalories' worth of a range of foods.

The students rated how full they felt every fifteen minutes, and could eat as much as they liked for two hours, watched by the research team. Taking the students' ratings and the observations into account, Dr. Holt's team assigned each food type a satiety score – white bread was given a 100 rating for comparison.

Confectionery and pastries came low on the scale (70 to 80), leaving the students feeling hungry again soon after eating. Potatoes (320), and fruit and vegetables in general (160 to 200), kept them satisfied longest.

Fiber filling

One satiating food type is fiber. A high-fiber diet will help you feel fuller for longer, leading you to eat fewer calories overall. It is also good for your health. Fiber is found in plant foods such as cereals, pulses, fruits, and raw or lightly cooked vegetables. It you want a slice of bread, choose high-fiber whole wheat bread – it has a much higher satiety index (157) than low-fiber white bread (100).

Fiber provides very few calories, but it adds bulk. When your stomach is empty it produces lots of ghrelin, which in turn makes the hypothalamus switch on your desire to eat. After eating a meal, your stomach wall is at full stretch and it stops producing ghrelin. Without ghrelin the hypothalamus turns off the "I feel hungry" switch.

Fiber also acts like a sponge, absorbing and holding on to water as it passes into the stomach. Foods that contain a lot of water can increase satiety. Water has absolutely no calories yet it adds volume to the food swelling up in your stomach. However, drinking a glass of water before a meal won't help fill you up because the stomach lets liquids pass straight through – it doesn't hold on to them as it does solid foods. Vegetables and fruits contain fiber and also contain around 90 percent water. Low-calorie soups are another great way to fill up: the water is mixed in with the food, so it should not pass straight through the stomach.

In addition, high-fiber foods generally take longer to chew. As well as helping you to feel more satisfied when you eat, this automatically slows down the speed at which you eat, giving your brain time to register the "stop-eating" hormone signals coming from the stomach. Finally, fiber stays in the stomach and small intestine longer because it is harder to digest. This in itself may send "I feel full" signals to the brain.

science jargon buster

Low-calorie satisfaction

Many nutritionists now focus on the "energy density" of different foods, in other words how many calories they contain per milliliter. Some foods – especially fatty foods – are very energy dense. They have loads of calories packed into a small volume. A teaspoon of olive oil and a plateful of vegetables contain a similar number of calories, but the plateful of vegetables will fill you up much more than the teaspoon of olive oil.

If you eat foods with high energy density, you will pile in the calories. If you eat less energy-dense foods you can eat more, feel full for longer and eat fewer calories overall.

Satisfying protein

Another key to staving off hunger for longer is protein. Foods rich in protein tend to be more satiating than fatty or carbohydrate-rich foods. Several studies into high-protein diets have found solid evidence that this nutrient can help to reduce appetite by making you feel satisfied. Protein-packed foods include lean meats, fish, beans, tofu and nuts.

Several diet plans have suggested eating lots of protein. The Atkins diet, once followed by nearly 10 percent of adults in the USA, is a high-protein diet where you can eat as much protein as you like, but almost no carbohydrates. Dr. Atkins' diet has been criticized for containing lots of fat and not nearly enough fruit and vegetables. Eating so much protein can also lead to kidney damage and a thinning of bones. But the Atkins diet does lead to dramatic weight loss, in the first few weeks at least. The satiating effect of protein may be part of the reason for its success.

Researchers at the University of Adelaide carried out a study into the effects of high-protein diets in 2003. The research involved fifty-seven people, all with similar age and build. The volunteers were split into two groups and put on to calorie-controlled diets. One group's diet consisted of a higher proportion of protein, but both groups consumed the same total number of calories. After twelve weeks, each group had lost about the same amount of weight, but the group with more protein in their diet reported feeling far fewer hunger pangs.

In a similar study at the University of Cincinnati, in 2005, a group of nineteen volunteers ate a relatively high-protein diet, but with no restrictions on how much they could eat. During the twelve-week study, the volunteers each consumed an average of 450 kilocalories less each day than they had before going on the high-protein diet, and lost an average of 5 kilograms (11 pounds). The researchers measured the concentration of leptin and ghrelin in the volunteers' blood. Amazingly, their leptin levels were low and ghrelin levels high – which would normally mean their brains would switch on feelings of hunger. But the participants reported feeling satisfied. The protein was somehow overriding the normal appetite signals.

No one is sure why protein is more satiating than other nutrients. But in 2006, the same researchers in Cincinnati announced that they had uncovered a potentially important clue. It came in the form of one of the building blocks of protein molecules, compounds called amino acids. Proteins are broken down into amino acids during digestion. The researchers found that an amino acid called leucine acts directly on the hypothalamus, and has an effect on appetite. Their research involved rats, but it is likely that the same effect is found in humans. In the experiment, rats that had received injections of leucine consumed one-third fewer calories than those that did not.

Several studies suggest that nuts can help to curb your appetite – and the protein effect is at least partly responsible (nuts are high in protein). In one study, at Purdue University, Indiana, people who snacked on 50 to 75 grams (2 to 3 ounces) of nuts each day experienced no extra weight gain compared with people who ate no nuts, despite a higher calorie intake. Another study, carried out in 2003 at the City of Hope National Medical Center in California, has suggested that eating nuts might actively help you to lose weight. The volunteers in the study were all given standard advice to help them lose weight. Half the subjects were asked to eat about 25 grams (1 ounce) of almonds every day, and lost more weight than the non-nut eaters.

Some researchers suggest that nuts might boost your metabolic rate, helping to burn off calories. And although nuts are naturally high in fat, it seems that this fat is not always well absorbed by the digestive system; the fact that people don't always chew nuts fully may also mean that not all the calories are consumed.

The science tests

Many dieters swear that drinking a glass of water before a meal reduces their appetites, and is therefore a real help in the mission to eat less. We put this idea to the test, with intriguing results. Another strategy that some people use to downsize their appetite is simply to take their time with a meal. The idea is that it takes time for appetite signals to reach the brain – so eating slowly should mean that you listen more closely to feelings of fullness.

Eating slowly
For our first study, we looked at whether eating slowly can make you eat less. Slow eating has been used in the treatment of obesity since the 1960s. Research about the effects of slow eating on appetite has been inconclusive. In 1997, for example, a study at Brighton University suggested that eating slowly actually increases appetite. A 2006 study, carried out by Dr. Corby Martin from the Pennington Biomedical Research Center in Louisiana, suggested that eating slowly makes you eat less. He also found that the effect is more pronounced in men than in women.

We asked Dr. Martin to help us with our own experiment. For our test, we took over the cafeteria of a busy bakery in London, and we worked with four of the employees there. We prepared lunch on two different days and controlled how fast our volunteers ate. At lunch, the food – bite-sized chunks of bread – was placed, with a jug of water, in the middle of the cafeteria table. Our volunteers were told to eat as much as they wished.

We ran the test on two days. On the first day, our volunteers could take a piece of bread as often as they liked. On the second day, however, they could only take a piece of bread when a laptop computer in the room produced a beep. On each day, the participants continued eating bread pieces until they were full.

Our results were inconclusive, not least because we only had four people taking part. Two of the participants ate slightly more, and the other two slightly less, when they were eating more slowly than normal.

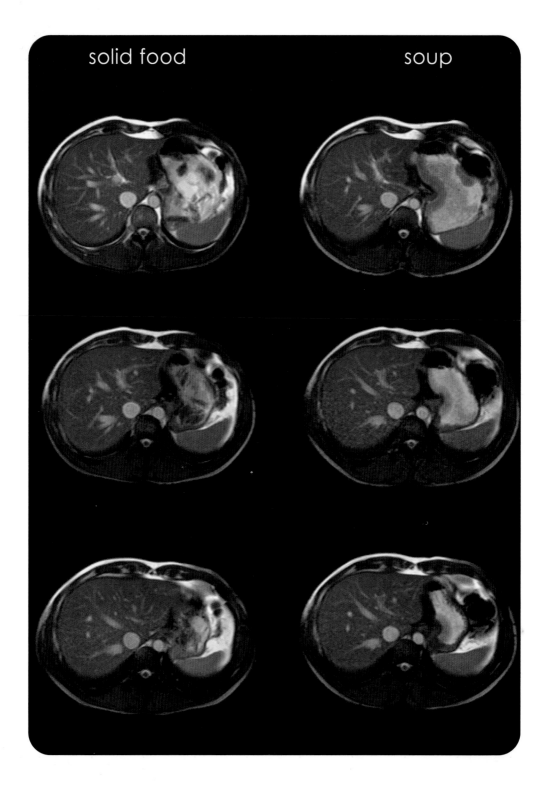

solid food

soup

Watering it down

Then we tested the idea that a glass of water before a meal will help you feel fuller for longer. Water has no calories, so if it can help to make you feel full sooner, it could really help. For this test, we worked with researchers at the University of Nottingham.

We recruited twenty volunteers, and prepared two different versions of the same meal for them. The meal consisted of chargrilled chicken, vegetables and mushrooms, with a small bottle of still water. In one version of the meal, all the solid elements were presented on a plate, and the water was drunk separately before they started eating. In the other version of the meal, all the ingredients were mixed together with the water and blended into a soup. We knew that pure water passes straight through the stomach, since there are no nutrients in it. But in the soup, the water is mixed in, and would be held back for a long time. So the souped meal would take up more space in the stomach, and we predicted that it would keep our volunteers feeling fuller for longer.

After eating the meals, our volunteers completed a questionnaire every forty-five minutes for three hours, which gave us an idea of how full they felt, and how long it would take before they felt they could eat again. And to get the inside story, the university researchers also took a series of MRI (magnetic resonance imaging) scans of three of our volunteers. The resulting images showed that the non-souped meal really did take up less space in the stomach.

This was a small study, involving one particular meal, so the results are not conclusive. But the questionnaires and the scans both support the idea that if you want to use water to make yourself feel full, and therefore eat less, it is probably a good idea to eat soup.

We compared two very similar meals, to see which would keep our volunteers feeling full for longer. The two meals had identical ingredients, but in one meal, the ingredients were combined together to make a soup. In the other, the water was drunk separately.

The MRI images on the facing page, produced at the University of Nottingham, follow the progress of the meals inside our volunteers' stomachs. The uppermost images show the meals just after consumption, the middle images forty-five minutes later, and the bottom images a further forty-five minutes later. The non-souped meal appears as chunks of food surrounded by liquid, while the souped meal appears as a continuous color, and takes up more volume for longer.

The soup secret

Low-calorie vegetable soup is one of the best-kept secrets of dieting. Snack on soup to turn the appetite signal off. The fiber and the water add bulk without adding calories, fill the stomach up and keep you feeling fuller for longer.

TOP TIPS – Satiety

Curb your appetite, and you will eat less. Remember:

1   Foods with low-energy density will satisfy your appetite with fewer calories:
    ✳ Look for high water content: soups, fruit and vegetables.
    ✳ Choose low-fat options, because fat contains the most calories.

2   High-fiber foods also bulk out in your stomach, making you feel full.
    ✳ Go for high-fiber foods: whole wheat foods, fruit and vegetables.

3   Protein-rich foods – such as lean meats, fish and nuts – can keep you feeling fuller for longer.
    The table below gives you the protein content of typical protein-rich foods. All portions on this
    table are equal to 150 calories. Choose these foods to help curb hunger.

Protein-rich food	Protein content (grams)	Portion size (all about the size of a pack of playing cards unless stated)
Yogurt, diet/low-calorie	16	365g (about 2 x 8oz cups)
Chicken roast (no skin)	25	220g
Steak – grilled, visible fat removed	26	252g
Fish – cod, skinless, grilled	33	158g
Tuna canned in water	35	150g
Nuts		
Hazelnuts	3	23g
Brazil nuts	3	22g
Walnuts	3	21g
Almonds	5	25g (small handful)
Peanuts (roasted)	6	25g

✳ Carry a small bag of almonds around as a snack, instead of chips or chocolate.

✳ Try a yogurt topped with nut-rich muesli for breakfast.

✳ Replace white bread with whole wheat bread.

✳ Use whole wheat pasta instead of white pasta.

✳ Increase portion sizes of vegetables on your dinner plate.

✳ Pile up the salad in your sandwich.

✳ Choose your favorite fruit or try vegetable sticks as a snack.

✳ Add extra vegetables to soups and stews.

✳ Have a side order of salad.

✳ Eat low-calorie vegetable soup as a starter – this WILL fill you up.

Why do we overeat?: portion size psychology

It should be simple: if you don't want to put on weight, don't eat more than you need. So why do so many of us consistently overeat?

Our bodies have several ways of telling us when we have had enough – but many of us ignore the signs and keep on eating. There are many reasons for this. Some are biological, perhaps left over from times way back in our evolutionary history when food was harder to come by. But research shows that psychology plays a major role, too.

Mind what you eat

There are many factors other than food's volume and energy content that determine how much we eat. For example, the temperature, color and ambient sounds in the surroundings in which we eat play a part. If we are distracted – deep in conversation or watching television, for example – we tend to eat more. Packaging or labeling of food can be very important. The shape and size of a container, even the name of a food can influence the way we perceive it: whether we like it or not, how much we are willing to pay for it –

and how much of it we consume.

Even simply being presented with a variety of food, rather than just a single type, can be a dieter's downfall. You know how at the end of the main course you've always got room for dessert, no matter how full you feel? There's no way you could eat another roast potato, but you could manage a small bowl of ice cream. Some people call this phenomenon "pudding tummy."

In fact, this may not be entirely due to psychology. Some nutritionists believe that we have a different appetite for each type of flavor, perhaps to ensure that we get a varied diet. If that is true, then in a world where food is so easily available, variety could really spell trouble for anyone trying to eat less. In one study, volunteers given six flavors of jellybeans consumed almost twice as many as those given just four. Variety in your diet is essential if you are to get all the nutrients you need. But within a particular meal, you have to be careful. If you are dieting, it might be a good idea to avoid buffets and tapas restaurants.

One of the most prominent researchers into the psychology of overeating is Professor Brian Wansink, the John S. Dyson Professor of

Marketing at Cornell University, New York State. In a series of fascinating experiments, Professor Wansink has uncovered many worrying eating behaviors. Most of his research, and similar work carried out by others, only focuses on eating behaviors during individual mealtimes. But there is plenty of evidence that if people eat more than they need at one meal, they don't often make up for it by eating less later on.

Don't go large

A double Whopper, a bucket-sized soft drink, a mountain of fries, and later at the movies a vast tub of popcorn. Bigger portions of fast food seem like great value: they only cost a little bit more than the regular size – and you can always leave some if you feel full up.

In 2005, to investigate what effect "going large" can have, Wansink hosted a movie night, during which he dished out free popcorn. The volunteer moviegoers were given either a medium (4-ounce) or a large (8-ounce) box of popcorn. In addition, some of the boxes contained popcorn that was stale, while in the other boxes the popcorn was freshly made.

Amazingly, the people who were given large boxes ate more than 45 percent more popcorn than those with medium boxes – taking in around 100 calories more. The effect even carried over to the stale popcorn, where those with the large portion ate more than 30 percent more than those with a medium box. Similar experiments, involving bags of candy munched while volunteers were watching television, and bowls of buffet snacks at parties, yielded similar results.

Wansink suggests that people subconsciously assume that a portion presented to them is of an appropriate size. Of course, you could turn this around, and serve healthy foods in larger portions. Big bowls of carrots or other raw vegetables could be the way forward when you're watching television or putting food out for a party.

The eyes have it

One of the strongest psychological motivations to eat more than we should seems to be the need to empty our plates. It may be a throwback to what we learned at the dinner table in childhood, or simply a dislike of waste. In 2005, Wansink published the results of a clever experiment he had carried out at his University campus.

Wansink set up four soup bowls at a table. The experiment's participants had been told that they would be trying out a new recipe for tomato soup, and that they should eat as much as they wanted. Unknown to the participants, two of the soup bowls were "bottomless": they were rigged with a device that allowed Wansink's research team to refill the bowl very slowly as the volunteers emptied it.

On average, the people eating from the self-refilling bowl ate a stunning 73 percent more soup than the others. However, they estimated that they had eaten about the same as the other participants, and they did not report feeling full.

In the bottomless soup bowl experiment, the visual cues are important: if the bowl is still full, you eat more. But in some cases, using your eyes can also make you eat less. If you are presented with an indication of how much you have already eaten. In another of Wansink's ingenious experiments, he found that people eat fewer sweets when the wrappers are left to pile up, and fewer chicken drumsticks when the bones are left behind.

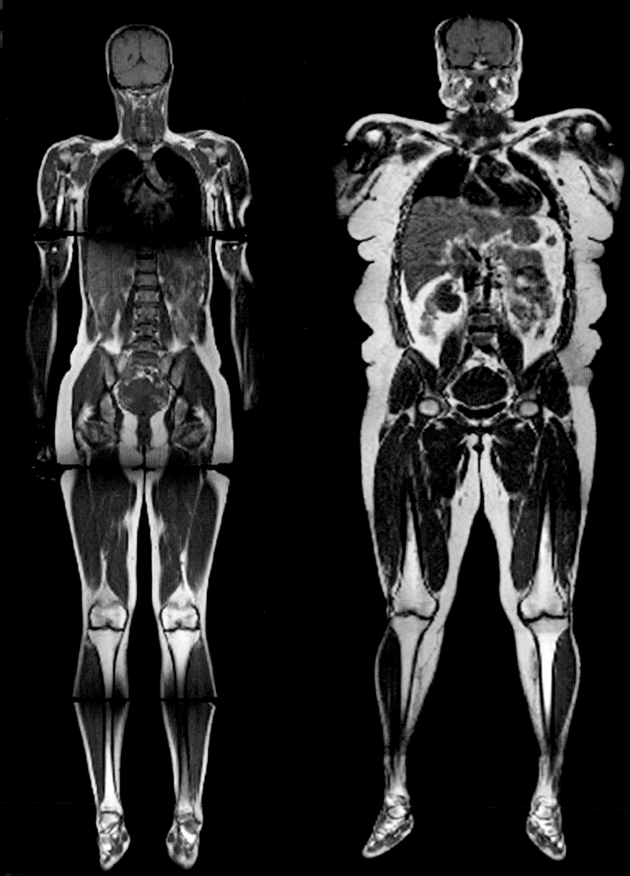

The science test

Will you eat less if you are reminded of how much you've already eaten? To find out, we laid on a banquet for a group of thirty Saxon reenactors, in our own version of Professor Wansink's chicken drumsticks experiment.

After a hard day's reenacting, they sat down to an eat-as-much-as-you-like banquet in which they were served chicken drumsticks. The volunteers were split into two groups, with an even distribution of weight, height and sex between them. The groups sat at two different tables, so that they could not easily see each other.

At one table, we made sure we cleared away the chicken bones as soon as they were finished. In that way, as the meal progressed, our volunteers weren't reminded of how much chicken they had already eaten. At the other table, we didn't clear the bones away – each person had their own plate in front of them, on which they left their bones. The two halves of the banquet were identical in every other respect. For each table, the chicken drumsticks were weighed before the meal, and the leftovers were weighed afterward. From the difference in weight, we calculated how much chicken each group had eaten.

We had predicted that having a visual reminder of how much our volunteers had eaten would help make them stop eating earlier. So we weren't surprised to find that the people whose chicken bones were left lying around ate 10 percent less.

TOP TIPS – You can eat less

We often eat more than our appetites would otherwise make us eat.

You can avoid this:
* Listen to your body telling you how much you need, rather than your conscience telling you to clean your plate.
* Keep track of what you've already consumed – don't get rid of chicken bones or candy wrappers right away, for example. Extend this idea over longer periods – keep a note, mental or written, of what you eat during the day.
* Presented with a variety of foods, we tend to eat more. If you are dieting, it might be a good idea to avoid buffets.
* Portion size often determines how much we eat. It is best not to go large, even though it is better value for money.

Most fat cells are located under the deepest layer of your skin. These remarkable images, taken by an MRI scanner, are "slices" through an overweight person (right) and a normal weight person. The subcutaneous fat has been colored yellow. But fat cells are also found around your internal organs – this has been colored green.

Are you overweight?

Body mass index (BMI):

$$BMI = \frac{weight \ (kg)}{height \times height \ (m \times m)}$$

Example: Height 1.55m (5ft 1in); Weight 65kg (10st 3lb)

Height x height = 1.55 x 1.55 = 2.4

BMI = 65 ÷ 2.4 = 27

To convert pounds to kilograms, divide by 2.2.

To convert inches to meters multiply by 0.0254

Use the following guide to work out whether you are a healthy weight.

BMI

Under 18.5	Underweight
19.0–24.9	Health weight
25.0-29.9	Overweight
Over 30	Obese

Waist circumference:

Carrying excess fat around your middle is linked to an increased risk of developing diabetes and cardiovascular diseases.

	Elevated risk	High risk
Men	94cm (37 inches)	102cm (40 inches)
Women	80cm (32 inches)	88cm (35 inches)

If you are overweight or obese or have a big waist circumference you need to take some positive steps to lose weight.

If you need to lose weight this might help you:

* First set yourself a realistic goal: aim to lose no more than 10 percent of your body weight.
* Once you've reached this goal, try to maintain this weight for a few weeks.
* Go for another 5–10 percent reduction if necessary.

Some practical dieting ideas:

1 Check portion sizes:

Reducing portion sizes reduces calories. Here are the recommended portion sizes.

Food type	Portion size per meal
Cooked rice, pasta, potatoes	2 to 3 tablespoons
Meat and fish	Size of a pack of playing cards
Breakfast cereals	3 tablespoons
Cheese	Size of a small matchbox
Fruit juices	1 small glass

2 Cut fat:

Fatty foods are high in calories. In the following table, each food on the left has the same calorie content as the corresponding food on the right.

High-fat food	Low-fat food
Large pat of butter (8g)	3 medium-sized boiled potatoes
Small cube of pork fat (5g)	2 tablespoons of egg noodles
1 teaspoon of olive oil	4 tablespoons (150g) of carrots
1 teaspoon of chocolate spread	28 raspberries (110g)

3 Stop those hunger pangs:

Fill yourself up with foods with low energy density, and high-fiber foods, and eat protein-rich foods to reduce appetite for longer.

4 Plan your meals and snacks:

People who successfully lose weight and keep it off use structured meal plans to help control their calorie intake. Regular meals, including breakfast and planned snacks, help to keep calorie intake under control.

5 Putting it all together

Here are some meal and snack suggestions to help you see how all the diet tips can work:

	Plan 1	Plan 2	Plan 3
Breakfast	Porridge made with semi-skimmed milk	Cooked breakfast, lean grilled bacon and scrambled egg	Nut rich muesli with yogurt
Mid-morning snack	Diet yogurt		
Lunch	Vegetable soup with whole wheat toast; piece of fruit	Tuna sandwich made with whole wheat bread; piece of fruit	Baked beans on whole wheat toast
Mid-afternoon snack		Handful of almonds	Diet yogurt
Dinner	Roast skinless chicken, with favorite vegetable and whole wheat pasta; diet yogurt and fruit	Grilled fish, side salad topped with a handful of nuts and rice	Grilled steak with favorite vegetables and baked potato
Evening snack			Fruit

SUMMARY: HOW TO BE SLIM

 THERE IS EVIDENCE THAT A DIET RICH IN CALCIUM, AND PARTICULARLY IN LOW-FAT DAIRY PRODUCTS, CAN HELP WITH WEIGHT LOSS.

 Your metabolic rate – how many calories you burn each day – depends upon your age and your sex, your level of physical activity, and your body weight. Contrary to popular belief, heavier people have higher metabolic rates than lighter people.

IT IS EASY TO IGNORE THE BODY'S APPETITE SIGNALS, ESPECIALLY WHEN EATING OUT: BEING DISTRACTED, BEING SERVED LARGE PORTIONS, AND BEING PRESENTED WITH A LARGE VARIETY OF FOODS CAN ALL MAKE US EAT MORE THAN WE NEED.

Understanding and controlling your appetite is crucial in an attempt to take in fewer calories. Certain foods will fill you up more than others for the same calorie intake.

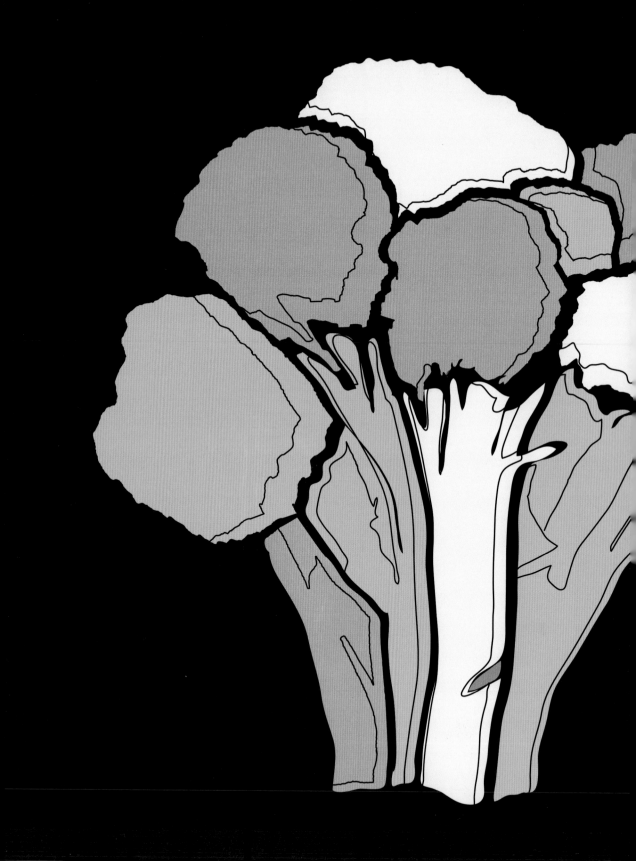

3. HOW TO FEED THE KIDS

HOW TO FEED THE KIDS

Miracles or monsters, kids are our pride and joy. They are the next generation, and what they eat now could safeguard or sabotage their health and happiness in later life.

As parents we want what's best for our precious ones – of course we do – so we conscientiously attempt to enforce ideal eating patterns on them, only to discover that we've bred very determined individuals with food preferences of their own, thank you very much. Nevertheless, how and what we feed our children really matters – even if they don't think so.

Children's physical and mental development depends upon them getting all the nutrients they need from a balanced, varied diet. What kids eat can affect their performance at school, their behavior and, of course, their health. We looked at the importance of a good breakfast, and whether what kids eat before the school day can make a difference to how they perform during it.

Too many children are growing up in ignorance or defiance of good nutrition. Some are happy snackers grazing all day, some just plain greedy and overweight. Childhood obesity is a major problem: statistics from the 2004 Annual Health Survey of Great Britain, published in 2006, show that 19 percent (nearly one-fifth) of all British children aged two to fifteen are obese. Since 1995, there has been a 10 percent increase in obesity in boys and a 15 percent increase for girls. And several studies show that overweight children have a much higher chance of becoming overweight adults.

One of the main reasons why so many children are becoming overweight, and even obese, is that they love to eat sugary and fatty foods – junk food, chocolate and chips. Why do we humans love these foods so much? And can we do anything to encourage children of all ages to try healthier alternatives?

We investigated the psychology behind snacks – for example whether hiding them away makes any difference – and we looked at why so many parents have trouble getting their children to eat their greens.

We also demonstrated how watching television while you eat can be bad for your children's waistlines. And we wondered why all children are not obese: do we have something inside us that tells us when we have eaten enough? And if we do, why doesn't it work in everyone? Along the way we wanted to explode a few myths, such as the idea that too many sugary snacks can change your children from serene angels to hyperactive little devils.

TOP TIPS – Kids and a healthy diet

These Top Tips apply to children two years and older. Children need a varied diet that provides enough energy and protein for growth and repair and contains all the essential vitamins and minerals.

Here are the basics:

* Carbohydrate-rich foods are a source of energy. Choose unrefined versions such as brown rice, whole wheat pasta, whole wheat or granary breads and breakfast cereals such as wheat biscuits, porridge and reduced-sugar muesli. These should provide about half your child's energy intake.
* Protein foods. Choose lean meats, fish, eggs, beans and pulses for growth and repair.
* Dairy foods provide calcium for healthy bones. Choose semi-skimmed milk, low or reduced-fat versions of yogurt and cheese.
* Fruit and vegetables provide vitamins and fiber. Aim to include as much as possible in your children's diet. Frozen and canned count as well as fresh.
* Fats and fatty foods; always use fats sparingly. Try to use more vegetable-based oils and spreads, rather than animal type fats. Keep fatty foods and snacks to a minimum.
* Keep sugary foods such as cakes, cookies, candy and chocolate to a minimum: they should be used as occasional treat foods.

Portion size:
knowing when to stop

Some children just don't know when to stop. This phrase may be truer than you think, at least when it comes to food. The same cannot be said of babies, who all seem to have an inbuilt sense of "portion control": they know when they have had enough. As we grow older, many of us seem to lose that ability. In the modern world, where we have practically unlimited access to sugary and fatty foods, the result is an epidemic of childhood obesity.

A growing problem

Around one-fifth of all school-age children in Britain are overweight. In the USA, the figure is one-third. These rates have almost tripled in the past twenty years. Overweight children are more likely to become overweight adults, and therefore have a significantly increased risk of developing diabetes, cancer and heart disease. Sadly, children who are overweight are also more likely to be bullied, because of their size. About 1 in 20 children is clinically obese, as defined by body mass index (BMI), a number worked out from a person's height and weight.

Many different factors contribute to childhood obesity. For example, children are more prone to becoming overweight if they were underfed in the womb; if they are from poorer families; if their parents smoke; if they are depressed; and if they take certain medications, such as steroids. Of course, the ultimate cause of obesity – for adults and children alike – is consuming more calories than the body needs. Taking regular exercise and eating fewer calories are the only effective ways to reduce the excess.

What makes some children eat more calories than they need? Genetics plays a part in about 5 percent of all cases of obesity. In other words, 1 in 20 obese children was born with an inability to sense when to stop eating. If this problem is identified early enough, doctors and nutritionists can intervene and help to manage the problem. Everyone else seems to be born with an inbuilt ability to gauge when they have eaten enough.

Our natural sense of "fullness" is

perfectly demonstrated by breastfeeding babies. They tend to stop feeding when they have had enough – and mothers are usually relieved when this happens. Many parents who bottle-feed, on the other hand, often encourage their babies to finish the entire contents of the bottle, regardless of how full the baby might feel. As a result, bottle-fed babies are more likely to become obese children, perhaps having learned to ignore the signals that tell them to stop.

Our inbuilt appetite signals are not restricted to the amount of food we consume. An experiment with bottle-fed babies showed that they are somehow able to sense when they have had enough calories. The experiment's researchers varied the caloric content of their milk and, amazingly, the amounts the babies drank varied accordingly – the more calories, the less they drank.

Various researchers have investigated children's and young adults' sense of when to stop eating. In each case, the more that was put in front of them, the more they ate. Some studies suggest that children listen to their bodies' appetite signals until about the age of three, while others suggest that children as young as two have lost touch with this important ability. In all cases, children were found to eat less if they served themselves – in other words, if they decided their own portion size.

TV dinners

Of all the factors involved in the growing problem of obesity, the habit of watching television seems to be one of the most important. One British study, by Dr. Russell Viner at the University College, London, published in 2005, monitored the television viewing patterns of nearly 11,000 people from their birth in 1970. A surprising finding was that the risk of adult obesity increased by 7 percent for every additional hour spent watching weekend television at five years old. And the more television people watched as children, the more sedentary their lifestyle became as adults.

The link between television viewing and childhood obesity is by no means confirmed. Some studies have found there is no link at all. But there are three very good reasons why watching television might play a part in childhood obesity.

First, watching a lot of television means spending long stretches of time sitting still. A study by the Harvard School of Health in 2006 found a clear link between time spent watching television and exercise levels. The researchers used pedometers to measure the number of steps taken per day by residents of Boston, Massachusetts. They found that for every hour of television watched, the participants took an average of 144 fewer steps each day. The average time the people spent watching television was 3.6 hours, and that made a potential difference of more than 500 steps per day. That number of steps uses a significant number of calories – especially when extended over a year. This research involved adults, but the finding – that the more time you spend watching television, the fewer calories you burn – probably applies equally to children.

The second way in which watching television may increase obesity is through advertising. A large proportion of commercials during children's programs are for snacks or other processed foods, or for fast-food outlets. There has been a ban on all television advertising aimed at under-12s in Sweden since 1991. And in Britain, there are several influential organizations pressing for a ban on junk-food advertising aimed at children. In 2006, the television industry watchdog, Ofcom, published a consultation document that proposed restrictions on the advertisement of "high fat, sugar and salt" food

and drink products. British advertisers have already cut down on the number of such ads, but they are understandably cautious about a ban: it is fair to assume that advertising has an effect on children's eating habits – otherwise it would quickly dry up.

Third, television is a distraction. We tend to ignore the signs of fullness while eating in front of the television – much more so than if we were eating with the television turned off. It is easy to munch our way through snacks, slowly but surely, while we watch a film or our favorite soap.

The science tests

We carried out our own experiments to investigate how well children listen to their appetite signals. First, we wanted to see if we could trick them into eating more food just by changing the sizes of their lunch portions. Then we tried to find out if watching television really can make children ignore their own bodies telling them they're stuffed.

Big portion, little portion

For our first experiment, we went along to a summer sports camp at an American school in England, to see if the children would ignore the "full" feeling and just keep eating. We provided lunch for a group of hungry five- and six-year-old campers on two days. There were eight children altogether. We were careful to keep everything the same on both days – except the size of the portions.

During each morning, we made sure the children were kept very busy – we put them through a series of physical activities that would make all of them very hungry. On the first day, we

asked the cafeteria staff to prepare and serve "normal" portions of Spaghetti Bolognese – weighed and calorie-counted to be a recommended lunch for children of that age. We worked with nutritionist Tanya Carr, who told us that children should obtain one-third of their daily calories from their lunch. She advised us what portion sizes to use.

On the second day, the cafeteria staff presented the children with the same meal, but the portions were twice the size and contained twice the number of calories. On both days we monitored how much food was left on the plates.

As you would expect, every child finished, or very nearly finished, his or her meal on the first day. On the second day, several of the children nearly cleaned the plate, and two plates were completely emptied. Overall, the children in our experiments ate 73 percent more Spaghetti Bolognese on the second day. All the children also ate dessert of cookies and fresh fruit.

Different portions

We made children eat more, just by serving them bigger portions.

To find out whether portion size can make a difference to how much kids eat, we presented eight children with meals on two different occasions. The meals were identical – Spaghetti Bolognese – but on the second occasion, we served up twice as much as the first time: twice the weight, twice the calories.

The first time we fed the children, we gave them the recommended amounts of food. They all finished their food and said they were full. Amazingly, when presented with twice as much, most of the children still finished their meals – and overall, 73 percent more food was consumed.

TOP TIPS – Managing children's portion sizes

Portion size is strongly habituated: we become used to eating bigger and bigger portion sizes yet still feel the same fullness. As portion sizes have increased, children have become conditioned to eating more calories than they need.

Downsize portions – if your child complains suggest they eat what they have first and if they are still hungry then they can have seconds. Space out the time between first and second helpings and they will probably feel less keen on insisting on seconds.

Children don't need as much as adults. Think twice when serving out meals, and make sure theirs is smaller than a typical adult's serving.

Avoid the supersize, kingsize, or "25% extra" foods; instead seek out the mini- and fun-size foods.

TOP TIPS – Too much TV?

- **Some sedentary behaviors, especially watching television, can increase food intake. Snacking at these times is likely to be on foods and drinks that are high in fat, salt and sugar.**
- **Turn off the television, get the children up and out riding their bikes, playing at the park or any activity they really enjoy doing.**
- **If your children demand snack food in front of the TV or computer screen try plain popcorn, vegetable sticks or slices of fruit.**

Eating to distraction

We conducted the second experiment over two evenings, in a family home. Our guinea pig was eleven-year-old Rosie. On each, we provided a plateful of pizza slices, Rosie's favorite food. Importantly, she had to serve herself. Each of the pizzas we cooked provided 696 kilocalories, and we cut the pizzas into nine slices each. We took the crusts off the pizza slices, so each one had about 75 kilocalories.

On the first evening, Rosie sat with her mother at the dinner table with the television turned on. Eating as she watched, Rosie took thirteen pizza slices. On the second evening, Rosie was presented with exactly the same food, but with the television turned off. This time, she took only ten slices.

So, Rosie took three slices more when she was watching the television. This is one-third of a pizza, or 225 kilocalories, more than when she was not watching. It is not a huge amount of food but, over a year it equates to about 120 pizzas!

Our experiments were by no means rigorous. The size of the children's appetites would have depended on how much they ate before the experiment, and how much exercise they had taken. But they do echo what many more thorough studies have already discovered: that it is easy for children to ignore their appetite signals and eat more than they need.

Food preferences:
accounting for taste

The dinner table can be a battlefield for parents. Even if you educate your children about the long-term benefits of a healthy diet, it seems that taste buds, peer pressure or just personal preference will win through in the end. Imagine the scenario: "Raw vegetables and dips or fries and ketchup, kids?" Most children eat fewer than two portions of fruit and vegetables per day, yet food agencies tell us that we should all have five.

Fortunately, you can influence your children's food preferences – even before they are born. Once they are older, you have to use a little psychology.

A matter of taste

Along with sight, the senses of taste and smell are the gatekeepers to our digestive system. They can save our lives: things that taste sweet are normally harmless sources of energy, for example, while things that taste bitter could be poisonous. Unfortunately, many vegetables stimulate our bitterness sensors, and this is largely why children don't like eating them.

At birth, most of us have an average of 10,000 taste buds, and at eighty years old only around 3,000 remain. But about a third of us are "supertasters" – born with something like three times as many taste buds as other people. Supertasters are more prone to disliking strong or unfamiliar flavors. The good news is that even supertasting children can overcome their bodies' prejudices against certain foods.

Many other factors can shape children's taste preferences. Perhaps most importantly, they are influenced by what their family eats and the flavors they are exposed to at an early age. This may be why people who grow up in an Asian family, for instance, are likely to develop a taste for spicy food. Parents can exploit this early shaping of children's palates by introducing a variety of foods to children when they are young, encouraging them to try new things. Also, when they go to school, they will begin to mix with children who like different foods – another opportunity to broaden their taste awareness.

But the training of the taste buds actually starts in the womb...

A taste of things to come

It is a shock to come out from the safe, warm and enclosed womb into the scary, cold and open world. Research has shown that memories from the womb can be important in comforting young babies. Perhaps the best example of this is a study in 1987 by Peter Hepper at Queen's University, Belfast. Hepper found that some babies calmed down whenever they heard the theme tune of the television soap opera *Neighbours*. The only babies who reacted in this way were those whose mothers regularly watched the show during pregnancy. Similarly, babies experience certain smells and tastes while they are busy growing in the womb, which can also be comforting in the world outside.

Suspended in its bath of amniotic fluid, a developing fetus comes into contact with chemicals that seep into the fluid from its mother's body. Its senses of taste and smell, though not fully developed, can detect some of those chemicals. From around twelve weeks into pregnancy, a fetus even swallows the amniotic fluid. And several experiments have not only confirmed that food flavors diffuse into the fluid, they also suggest that those flavors can influence the baby's food choices for years to come.

In 1995, Peter Hepper tested the reaction of babies just twenty hours old to the smell of garlic. Half of the mothers in the experiment had eaten garlic at least four times each week in the late stages of pregnancy, while the other half had not eaten any. The babies whose mothers had eaten no garlic turned away from the smell, while the others did not mind it. Another study, in France, used a drink flavored with anise – the spice plant whose fruits are aniseed – instead of garlic, with very similar results.

If food flavors can make it into the womb and influence babies' taste preferences, what happens after the baby is born? When you are breastfeeding can the food you eat affect breast milk, and whether or not your baby will like particular food flavors? In 2001, Julie Mennella and her colleagues at the Monell Chemical Senses Center in Philadelphia, Pennsylvania, carried out a fascinating study that clearly demonstrates that it can.

The team recruited some mothers-to-be and divided them randomly into three groups. One-third of the mothers drank carrot juice regularly only during pregnancy; a second group drank carrot juice regularly only during the months they were breastfeeding; a third group drank no carrot juice at all. When the babies were weaned on to solid foods, they were given carrot-flavored cereal to try. The babies who had experienced the flavors of carrot juice in the womb or in breast milk took to the cereal much better than those that had not.

What's the take-home message for parents who care about their children's diets? By eating vegetables and other healthy food during pregnancy, mothers-to-be can give their unborn baby a head start in developing good eating habits. And by breastfeeding they can continue that process. My daughter hates fish. At two years of age she would even spit out fish fingers. I sometimes wonder: if I had eaten more fish when I was pregnant, would she now have a taste for this wonderful, healthy food?

The tongue takes up blue food coloring, but taste buds don't – the boy on the right has many more taste buds than the boy on the left – he is a "supertaster." Children who are supertasters tend to be fussy eaters, because they experience the bitterness of vegetables like broccoli more intensely than other children. About 35 percent of girls and 15 percent of boys are supertasters.

New habits

If your children are no longer babies, but rampaging, broccoli-hating junk-food lovers, don't worry: all may not be lost. There are ways to get them to try new, healthy foods without having to force-feed them or even raise your voice. It's all a matter of psychology.

Many children are "neophobic" – they have a fear of new things. When it comes to food, this can be a real problem. Nearly all children have some neophobic tendencies. Fighting against them is not the best idea. We all know that if you tell children to do one thing, they will probably do the exact opposite. The more you tell them it's good for them, or that they must eat it, the less likely they are to have it. You need to employ more subtle approaches ... it's for their own good, after all.

Children's acceptance of new foods will increase if they see people around them enjoying them. As a parent, you can be an important dietary role model. In other words, they've got to see you eating healthy foods with gusto. But the effect is more potent if it is people their own age they see. We all know how easily children pick up *bad* habits from friends of their own age. But we can turn that around. Positive role models work, too, and not just other people's children but brothers and sisters as well. Some researchers

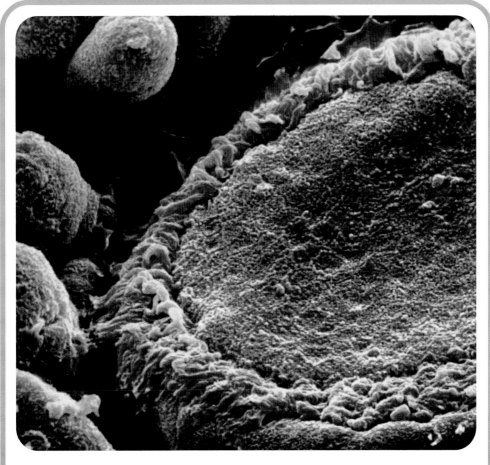

Scanning electron micrograph of a single taste bud, magnified 1,200 times

Taste buds

❋ Most taste buds are on the tongue, but they are also found in other parts of the mouth. A typical taste bud contains between 50 and 100 cells, each sensitive to chemicals in food.

❋ Taste buds give us five distinct taste sensations: sweet, salty, sour, bitter and umami. This last one has only recently been recognized in the West. It corresponds to the flavor of a natural chemical called glutamate found in highly "savory" foods like mushrooms, processed cheese and bacon, and an additive called monosodium glutamate common in Chinese cuisine. Scientists in China also recognize "pungent" as a flavor that our taste buds can recognize.

❋ Contrary to popular belief, every taste bud can detect each type of flavor – there is no such thing as a taste bud for sweet, one for sour and so on.

have managed to change what foods children like in just this way.

Another proven strategy is to introduce novel and healthy foods little by little. The first couple of times the child is served with broccoli, say, they might simply be encouraged to smell it and play with it. When children are under no pressure, they are likely to become curious about what broccoli might taste like (especially when they see you happily chomping on it). Research shows that it can take eight or more exposures before a child accepts a food like broccoli. Introduce the food in small amounts, perhaps a few days apart. It's a hassle, but it will be worth it in the long term.

The science test

There is hope for frustrated parents with children who are fussy eaters: studies show that you can influence children's taste preferences. We wanted to see the effects for ourselves. We went to a school in London to see if we could get some six- and seven-year-olds to start liking vegetables.

We sent a group of child actors into the school – all slightly older than the children in our chosen class. The visitors had all been on television and taken part in model photo-shoots. Importantly, we only chose actors who liked vegetables. After giving our class a talk about their exciting experiences in filmmaking and the modeling business, the visitors sat down to eat school lunch with the other children. Lunch was chicken, sausages, creamed potato, peas, carrots and broccoli. We asked the visiting children to eat lots of broccoli, and to talk enthusiastically about it if possible. Watched carefully by our hidden cameras, children who had previously refused point blank to go anywhere near broccoli were sniffing it, picking it up and showing an interest. Some were even quite happily munching away.

You can't have film stars around to your house to encourage your children to eat broccoli, but this experiment does show that children's taste preferences are not set in stone. And you can be a role model yourself – if you like broccoli, that is.

TOP TIPS – Getting children to try new foods

1 **Use non-food rewards:**
   Offering pudding as a reward for eating their greens reinforces the idea that vegetables are unpleasant and something to be endured rather than enjoyed.

   Try offering non-food rewards for good eating and good behavior. Star charts and stickers can motivate children. Collecting an agreed number of stars can add up to a reward such as a toy, a trip to a favorite park, or to the movie theater.

2 **Keep offering new foods, again and again:**

It is quite common for a child to be suspicious of a new food. Rejection is almost automatic. Parents often give up after a couple of refusals. Eventually the list of hardly tried "don't like" foods grows longer and longer while the accepted food list dwindles into a nutritional nightmare.

Studies also show that children are influenced by seeing their parents, carers and peers eating and enjoying the same foods. So get your dinner plate in order and tuck into the foods you want your children to eat too.

Keep calm and keep going with "stress-free" repeated offerings of the same food. If it gets rejected again, take it away without saying anything, leave it a week or so and try again.

Restricted access:
do you hide the cookies?

Surveys show that most children snack at least two or three times every day, and those snacks contribute about 25 percent of their total energy intake. Children love sweets and chips and all those other snacks that you want to keep as occasional treats. If your children keep picking at them whenever your back is turned, you have probably thought about putting them under lock and key – the food, not the children. Out of sight and out of mind, right? Not so, say psychologists: hiding something away will only make them want it more.

We explored this idea – by trying to make a bunch of four-year-olds go crazy for raisins.

Food dilemma

The sorts of foods that children love the most are the ones you find in brightly colored packages that say "buy me and make your child happy." But these foods are usually the ones that are sugary, fatty and salty – or at the very least, harmless but of no nutritional value. If your children gobble these foods all day, they can ruin their appetite and cost you a fortune. And yet you don't want to deny your children their pleasures. So you buy some anyway. And in all honesty, you probably want some for yourself, too.

When you get back from the store, you put these foods into the cupboard, fairly high up, so that the kids can't get at them whenever they want. You hope that by putting them out of sight – and by restricting your child's access to them – they might forget they exist and be pleasantly surprised when you bring them out as a treat.

Bad move! Restricting access to something can focus attention on it and make it seem even more special. Experiments with rats illustrate this effect. In one test, when rats were given access to an alcoholic drink for just twenty minutes every day, their consumption of alcohol actually went up compared with rats who had free access to it. Children are not rats – but they can behave in similar ways when access to a particular food is restricted.

Obviously you can't give alcohol to children in the name of science. Instead, researchers at Pennsylvania State University in the USA used peach- and apple-flavored cookies. During their experiment, a class of children became fans of the peach cookies, and remained indifferent about the apple ones. The only difference between the two – apart from the flavor – was that the peach cookies were in a closed jar so the children couldn't get at them. The jar was opened for two minutes during regular twenty-minute sessions over five weeks. There were plenty of apple cookies, in an open bowl, which the children could take at any time.

The "restricted" peach cookies in the jar soon became like gold dust. The children spoke about them much more than the apple flavor ones, and asked for them more often. They even tried to raid the jar when the researchers weren't looking.

The flavors were reversed in another group of children – and this time it was the apple cookies that became the big hit. The amazing conclusion of this experiment is that by restricting a child's access to a particular food, you make that food more desirable, just like the alcohol and the rats.

Through interviews with the children's parents, the researchers came to another conclusion: the more the parents hid the snacks at home, the more likely the children were to be overweight. Bizarre as this may sound, other studies have reported exactly the same phenomenon.

This whole business sounded so intriguing we simply had to see if we could observe the same thing.

The science test

Research has shown that restricted access to certain foods can make those foods more desirable to children. This can be negative when the restricted foods are sugary snacks, but we wanted to turn it around and encourage children to develop a liking for something healthier.

For our own experiment, we asked a the staff and pupils at a preparatory school for their help. Our guinea pigs were a class of eighteen four- and five-year-olds at a school in South London. Just as other experimenters had done previously, we needed to start by finding two foods that the children neither loved nor hated. We began by asking the children to rate a selection of snack items.

Rather than go for sugary, salty snacks, which the children would probably love anyway, we presented them with a selection of raisins, dried apple, dried mango, dried apricots, dried bananas, freeze-dried strawberries and prunes. Besides, we had to remain on the right side of the school's healthy eating policy. We asked the children to rate how they felt about a range of snacks using a chart of happy-, indifferent- and sad-looking faces. We gave points to each symbol – ten for happy, five for indifferent, zero for sad. When we added up the points, raisins and dried mango came out the best suited.

Each day, for a fortnight, just before morning break, the children had twenty minutes of "snack time." We set out the two snacks in bowls. The teacher blew her whistle to tell the children they were allowed to eat dried mango for fifteen minutes – but they were not allowed to eat the raisins. After ten minutes, the teacher blew the whistle for a second time, after which the children were allowed to help themselves to the raisins as well, for the remaining five minutes.

After two weeks of this regime in the children's daily snack time, we interviewed the children again to find out which snack the they preferred. Of the eighteen children, eleven preferred raisins, and seven liked mango best. At the beginning of the experiment, six children had rated mango and raisin equally – but by the end of the two weeks, those same children all preferred the raisins.

It's difficult to know how best to deal with this phenomenon. If hiding the unhealthy snacks is going to make them more desirable, what are you supposed to do? Giving your children free access to them is not likely to curb their consumption either. You could try using psychology to encourage your kids to crave healthy foods. It seems to work for raisins.

TOP TIPS – Food bans?

❋ Banned foods help to create a desire for forbidden treats. Allow all foods but remember that some are healthier than others. Children need to learn that foods such as cakes, chips, sweets and sugary drinks should be enjoyed only occasionally.

❋ Keep treats for parties or holidays, and only offer artificially sweetened or reduced-fat versions rather than a supersize full-sugar or full-fat version, in small portions.

Power breakfasts: glucose and the brain

It's eight o'clock on a school-day morning and the usual mix of panic and bad moods reign around the kitchen table. Charlie's lost his homework. Alex has lost her gym bag. Now it's too late for breakfast – again. So you just get them out through the door. They can survive until lunch. But wait a minute. Isn't breakfast a key meal, maybe the most important of the day? Is skipping breakfast such a good idea?

We set out to discover exactly how important breakfast really is – in particular for children who are going to school. We suspected it could enhance their ability to learn, concentrate and remember – and basically get their brains in gear for a morning at school.

Feeding the brain

The brain is a high-energy organ. Despite making up only about 2 percent of your body's weight, it consumes up to 20 percent of your total energy supply. When you're sleeping, the brain can account for two-thirds of your energy expenditure. That's a lot of energy – and things that use a lot of energy need a lot of fuel.

The brain's fuel is a type of sugar called glucose. It is the main fuel used by all the body's cells, but unlike other cells, brain cells cannot turn to other types of fuel – they depend upon glucose. After eating some carbohydrate-rich food – like cereal or bread – your body leaps into action and breaks the carbohydrates down into glucose. The glucose seeps into your bloodstream and is pumped around the body. But rather than allowing levels of sugar in your blood to rocket after a meal, your body ensures that levels stay the same, day and night. It does this by releasing a hormone called insulin into the blood.

Insulin causes cells – mainly in the liver and in muscles – to convert blood glucose to another chemical, called glycogen, and store it for use later. So as soon as the amount of glucose in your blood starts to rise, your body begins to stash some of it away in your liver and your muscles. The production of insulin shuts off when the concentration of glucose falls to a near-normal level – for a short while after a sugary snack, your blood glucose drops a little low. But it quickly gets back to normal: the cells containing glycogen now begin producing glucose again. This process ensures we always have the right concentration of glucose in the blood: the body is always either storing glucose away (as glycogen) or drawing on its energy reserves (of glycogen) in the muscles and liver to release glucose.

Science fact: blood glucose

About 5 grams (one teaspoon) of glucose is dissolved in your blood at all times – even when you haven't eaten any sugar for hours.

The amount of glucose available in your blood would keep you alive for less than an hour – and only about ten minutes if you were exercising heavily. The glucose stored in your liver could keep you alive for about two or three hours – glucose from the muscles, between ten and twelve hours. After that, you have to start using up your body's fats and proteins to keep your glucose level stable. This is why people in the late stages of starvation literally "waste away."

Breaking the fast

What about when you wake up in the morning – when you haven't eaten for, say, twelve hours? Are you wasting away? Can you survive until lunchtime without eating? And more importantly, will your children's brains be able to work efficiently if they miss breakfast?

Hang on, I hear you cry, we've all missed breakfast at least once in our lives and lived to tell the tale. Obviously we can manage. But by mid-morning, your stomach starts gurgling, it feels empty and wants some food. These hunger pangs might well affect a child's performance at school, but what about their glucose reserves? In theory the body will keep the glucose level constant for hours, even days to come, so skipping breakfast shouldn't affect the fuel supply to the brain.

And does the kind of food you eat for breakfast matter? Well, different carbohydrates break down into glucose at different rates. Sugars, for instance, are simple carbohydrates that can be broken down very quickly. Starch and other "complex" carbohydrates break down more slowly, releasing glucose into the blood over several hours. This means that less insulin is produced, and there is no need for the body to store the glucose away and retrieve it. Glucose from these foods is released at about the rate your body needs it. Sugars, releasing glucose rapidly, are said to have a high glycemic index, or "GI," while complex carbohydrates like starch, releasing glucose more slowly, have a low GI.

We wanted to find out if foods of different GIs might have an effect on our children's bodies – and their brains – during that crucial period between breakfast and lunch. Would low-GI foods be the better fuel, releasing glucose gradually over the course of the morning? Or would it be better to have a burst of glucose from sugary foods soon after breakfast, so that the body and brain have enough to keep them going? Would both be better than having no breakfast at all?

Before we could start, we needed to see if anyone else had got there before us. In the USA, about 10 million kids eat breakfast at school, compared with virtually none in Britain. The US School Breakfast Program began in 1966 to help ensure that children from low-income households got a proper breakfast. Studies carried out since then have shown that the program encourages pupils to turn up at school, on time, and can significantly improve school performance. But how much has this got to do with keeping children's brains fueled with a steady supply of glucose?

Several researchers have focused on whether missing breakfast reduces children's brainpower through the morning. The results have been very mixed. In kids who are undernourished or from poor families, breakfast really does seem to improve things such as reaction times and memory. But in most studies, children who are not undernourished showed no ill effects from missing breakfast. The studies have been done in a number of different countries: Jamaica, Sweden, South Africa, Chile and Peru. A few were carried out in the USA, but only one in the UK. And no one seemed to have compared low-GI and high-GI breakfast foods.

We were keen to do our own serious study of the effects of different breakfasts on those glucose-hungry brains we send off to school every morning. We asked Professor David Benton, of Swansea University's Psychology Department, to come onboard with us. Professor Benton has carried out research before into the relationship between people's diet and their mood and mental ability. But our research was completely new.

The science test

We wanted to find out if what kids eat for breakfast can make any difference to their mental abilities later in the morning. So over the course of three days, we provided the meals at a breakfast club in a school in Swansea. We worked with a single class of six- and seven-year-old children.

Each morning we provided three different breakfasts: one was a high-GI meal, one medium and one a low-GI meal. The three different breakfasts would supply glucose into the blood at different rates during the morning. We labeled the three different meals "American," "British" and "German" because of the food types they contained – see the table for details. All three meals provided about the same number of calories in total – although few children finished their meals. We measured how much each child left behind, so that we could estimate the number of calories he or she had consumed.

Nineteen children attended the breakfast club, which ran from 8:15 until 8:45 a.m. each day. Over the course of the three days, the children alternated which breakfast they ate, so that each child had each breakfast once. Perhaps not surprisingly, the American breakfast was the most popular, and some children did not like the German one at all.

Between 10:45 and 11:15 a.m. on each day, we ran a series of brainpower tests. The first was a frustration test using a simple electronic game of bat-and-ball, or TV tennis. We made the game very difficult; we wanted to see how they would respond to the frustration, not how well the children could learn the game. How patient could they be?

Next we tested memory: the children were given a card with pictures of twenty objects, which they looked at for forty seconds. Then they had sixty seconds to recall as many objects as possible (a test of verbal memory), and to place the objects in the correct positions on a blank card (spatial memory).

The third test measured the children's ability to concentrate on a particular task. It involved a machine with a buzzer and a light. Three seconds after the buzzer sounded, the light switched on – the children had to press a button as soon as they noticed it change. But sometimes the light did not light up until twelve seconds after the buzzer sounded. This delay meant that children whose minds wandered off easily would do badly on this test.

Professor Benton carried out a full mathematical analysis of the results, looking for any relationship between the kind of breakfast eaten and the children's performance. He estimated how much protein, carbohydrate and fat each child had consumed, and searched out any links between nutrients and performance. But we were particularly interested in the effect of the rate at which the carbohydrates were supplying glucose. The results were intriguing, although not altogether conclusive.

In the TV tennis game, the children who had eaten the high-GI breakfast performed noticeably worse than those who ate the low- and medium-GI meals – but only on the first day. On the other two days, there was no noticeable difference: this makes sense when you consider that by the second day, all the children knew that the task was frustrating, and gave up much sooner.

In the memory test, the children who had eaten high-GI breakfasts actually performed slightly better. But in the concentration experiment, the children who ate the high-GI breakfast had more lapses of concentration than the other children.

Generally, our results pointed to the advantages of a slow release of glucose through the morning, as a result of having a low-GI breakfast. But there was no great difference – a finding that is in line with previous studies.

Power breakfasts?

These are the three meals we provided at the breakfast club in Swansea:

"AMERICAN" BREAKFAST
HIGH GI – releases glucose rapidly.
Cornflakes (25g)
Milk (semi-skimmed, 115 ml)
Sugar (1 spoonful)
1 waffle
Jam

"BRITISH" BREAKFAST
MEDIUM GI – releases glucose more slowly.
Scrambled egg (60g)
Bread (1 slice)
Low-fat spread
Jam
Low-calorie yogurt

"GERMAN" BREAKFAST
LOW GI – releases glucose gradually.

Ham (1 slice, 30g)
Cheese (40g)
Rye bread
Low-fat spread

Eat breakfast

Nutritionists agree that breakfast is an important meal of the day. No one is going to starve to death if they skip breakfast, and their attention and other mental abilities through the day are not greatly affected without it. But eating regular meals is a great way to control your food intake – adult or child.

Any breakfast is better than none – but a low-GI breakfast seems to be best. Nutritionists suggest that low-GI foods are generally better than high-GI foods. There is strong evidence that eating high-GI foods contributes to obesity, for example. With so much glucose released into the bloodstream so quickly, the body stores much of it away, and is ready to receive more food if more is coming. Unfortunately, high-GI foods tend to taste sweeter and, as we saw in our experiment, that makes them more popular with most children. It might be a tough call to get your kids to eat low-GI porridge and muesli.

Around the world

If your kids still resist the low-GI breakfast, you could threaten them with these brain-power breakfasts from around the world:

Japan	**Miso soup, raw fish, raw egg on rice, pickled vegetables**
Egypt	**Slow-cooked beans or lentils in olive oil, lemon & garlic**
China	**Rice congee (a kind of porridge), soy milk, turnip cakes**

TOP TIPS – Energizing your children

❋ Children need a regular supply of energy; structured meals and snacks help provide this. If meals and snacks are planned, they are more likely to be healthier choices.

❋ Breakfast is an important meal. After a night's sleep, our bodies have just about used up their glucose store. Our brain functions exclusively on glucose, so breakfast helps us top up on brain fuel.

❋ Try carbohydrate foods that are digested and released slowly into the blood. Sometimes called low glycemic index (GI) foods, these carbohydrates provide a steady supply of fuel over the morning:

❋ Porridge or muesli are low GI, mini-shredded wheat make a good runner-up in the GI stakes.

❋ For toasting, choose whole wheat breads which have the highest content of intact grains. Add baked beans for an easy cooked breakfast.

❋ Fresh fruit, try with yogurt or put on top of breakfast cereal.

TRUTH ABOUT FOOD NO. 5:

SUGAR CAN'T MAKE CHILDREN HYPERACTIVE, BUT IT CAN MAKE THEM OVERWEIGHT.

TRUTH ABOUT FOOD NO. 6:

WE DEVELOP SOME OF OUR TASTE PREFERENCES WHEN WE ARE STILL IN THE WOMB.

Sweet things:
are kids mad for sugar?

You're organizing a party for your child's friends. What kind of things should you lay on for them? Well, you want them to have a great time so you get in foods they are bound to enjoy. A fine selection of colorful cakes, a plate of sandwich cookies, a bowl of chocolates, some sugary soft drinks, and ice cream to finish.

But wait a minute. Most parents assume that children plus sugary foods equals raucous and uncontrollable behavior. Those foods will strike fear into their hearts: the dreaded "sugar high." You can almost see the look of horror on their faces. You can't do that to them.

A child can easily consume the equivalent of twenty or thirty teaspoonfuls of sugar at a typical kids' party. But then again, it is a party, so you simply have to have a selection of sugary treats.

You may not have to worry: according to nutrition experts, the belief that children experience a "sugar high" is a myth.

Not all at once

We all know that sugar is a ready supply of energy. The sugar in most sugary foods is sucrose, which quickly and easily breaks down in the gut into glucose, which is the brain's fuel. It stands to reason that eating large quantities of sugary foods will give you boundless energy, doesn't it?

Just as we tell our kids not to eat their sweets all at one time, your body doesn't use up its sugar all at once. If there's more glucose available, the body doesn't use it more quickly, it squirrels some away to have later. Our bodies are very good at keeping blood glucose levels pretty constant. If you stuff yourself with sugar-rich food your blood glucose level will rise slightly and temporarily, but it will soon be back to normal.

Even if your blood glucose level is slightly higher than normal, your brain doesn't start working faster or going out of control. There is no accelerator pedal: brain cells only really have one speed. You can't "overdrive" them. So if kids consume lots of cakes and chocolates at a party, they may feel full, even sick, but it won't make them hyperactive.

But we've all seen it: our children can be little nightmares when we pick them up after a party. Psychologists' explanation for this is that kids' parties are exciting events, something out of the ordinary. Kids meet other children, they play games. There might be an entertainer – balloon animals, puppet shows or magic tricks are enough to make anyone feel a bit energized.

Of course, children might get "chemically energized" in other ways. Some sweet food and drinks contain other substances that really can act as stimulants. For example, chocolate and some sweet soft drinks contain caffeine, and some food additives have been linked to hyperactivity.

According to Dr. Richard Surwit at Duke University, North Carolina, the myth of the sugar rush may have begun during World War II. Dr. Surwit has noted that during the war, when sugar was scarce, the US government tried to reduce demand by informing everyone that sugar is bad for you and can cause hyperactivity.

Dr. Surwit has conducted careful studies examining what sugar intake can do to the brain and the mind. He monitored sugar intake, blood glucose levels and behavior – and he found no hyperactivity effect. Several other studies have come to the same conclusion.

But the myth of the sugar high is so ingrained in our culture that we just had to investigate it for ourselves.

The science test

We wanted to test whether sugar really makes children furiously energetic as so many people assume, but we also wanted to test parents' perceptions of their children's behavior. So, we held two carefully orchestrated children's parties.

The first was a classic high-energy romp. We invited a children's entertainer, whose enthusiasm would be infectious. There were games and there was music. But there was hardly any sugar. When the parents dropped off their children, they saw plates of sugar-rich goodies that they assumed were to be consumed during the party. We quickly hid them away as soon as the parents disappeared.

Two weeks later, the same group of children went to our second party. This was an altogether calmer affair. There were storytellers and quiet classroom-style activities. The children made cakes and fish costumes. But this time there was a selection of sugary foods – presented in a sober fashion, but deliciously sugary nonetheless. This time when the parents dropped off their children they saw no sugary foods – only a healthy lunch. Again, we removed the healthy lunch the moment they left.

How did the children's behavior differ

What are sugars?

Any ingredient ending in "-ose" listed on a food label is a sugar. The most common ones are sucrose, glucose, fructose and galactose. Plants manufacture glucose – from carbon dioxide and water – whenever sunlight shines on their leaves. Glucose is an example of a "monosaccharide," the simplest type of sugar. Plants can join two monosaccharides together to form disaccharides such as sucrose, or join hundreds together to from polysaccharides such as starch.

after the two parties? After the first one, all of the children were indeed hyped-up, full of energy, even badly behaved – despite the fact that they had consumed virtually no sugar at lunch. After the second party they were much quieter, even though they had consumed lots of sugary foods.

The conclusion was clear: the sugar made no difference to the children's behavior, which instead had been influenced by what was going on around them.

What about the parents' perceptions of their children's behavior? After each party we asked them to rate, out of 10, how much their children had been affected by their intake of sugar. As you might expect, they gave very high values after their children had been to the first party, and consistently lower values after the second one. And when we interviewed them they really seemed to believe that the manic behavior of their children after the first party had been entirely due to the sugar.

So if you're organizing a children's party, or if you're taking your kids to one, don't worry about the sugar. Let them eat cake. Let them fill up on jelly candies, cookies and soft drinks.

Of course, we're only talking about special occasions. There's nothing wrong with the occasional treat, but there is strong evidence that eating sugary foods all day and every day contributes to tooth decay and obesity, diabetes and heart disease.

TOP TIPS – Ditch the sugary snacks

Try these swaps for a healthier choice

Avoid	Try instead
Sugar-rich drinks	Water, reduced-fat milk or artificially sweetened drinks
Sweets	Chopped fruit or a handful of dried fruit
Chocolate	Yogurt
Sweet cookies	Carrot and cucumber sticks
Cake	Raisin bread
	Rice cakes with savory spread such as a yeast extract
	Breakfast cereal with semi-skimmed milk
	Fruit segments in artificially sweetened sugar jelly

HOW DO I GET MY CHILD TO EAT HEALTHY FOOD?

We have a special responsibility to feed our kids well: bad eating habits often endure into adulthood. But good habits endure, too. Introducing children to healthy eating is a precious gift. But we are often met with resistance. Many kids are fussy eaters – unwilling to try new foods, and eager to gorge themselves on junk food, chocolate and soft drinks.

One of the tried and tested ways of encouraging children to change a particular behavior is to use reward charts, and it can really help you to help your child eat more healthily. Of course, if your child is more than just a fussy eater or a snacker – and you think they may have a real problem, such as serious overeating or a severe lack of variety in their diet – then you should consult your physician.

A reward chart can simply be a piece of paper with a series of boxes on it – although you can make it more elaborate or decorative, or even buy one ready-made. A child earns a sticker whenever he or she behaves in a desired way – say, eating five portions of fruits and vegetables on a particular day.

When your child collects a certain number of stickers –

perhaps a week's worth – he or she gets a reward. The reward should not be food – especially not junk food or sugary snacks. Instead, plan activities that you and your child can do together – something they will look forward to and remember afterward.

REWARD CHART RULES

1. Before you start using a reward chart, discuss why you would like the child to adopt a new behavior, and make sure they understand how the system works – and what the reward will be.

2. Decide what you would like to change about your child's eating habits. It is important to be realistic – don't expect miracles.

Here are some desirable behaviors that a reward chart could help your child to achieve: eat a healthy breakfast; eat the evening meal at the table, with the television turned off; try new, healthy foods, such as broccoli; eat brown rice or whole wheat bread, instead of white rice and white bread; eat five portions per day of fruit and vegetables; burn off calories by taking regular exercise; have dried fruits rather than chocolates or sugary sweets.

3. Use one chart for each behavior you want to change – and only use one chart at a time.

4. Always remain positive, even on the occasions when you can't offer a sticker or a tick. Never remove a sticker or get rid of a tick. Help and advise children, and praise them often.

Star chart ★ ★ ★ ★ ★ ★ ★ ★ ★

	Breakfast
Monday	
Tuesday	
Wednesday	
Thursday	
Friday	
Saturday	
Sunday	

Lunch	Evening meal

SUMMARY:
HOW TO FEED THE KIDS

Children tend to ignore their appetite signals when they are distracted by the television; they also eat more if they are presented with larger portions.

IT IS NATURAL FOR CHILDREN TO BE FUSSY EATERS; TASTE BUDS HAVE EVOLVED TO MAKE US WARY OF NEW, BITTER FLAVORS.

Hiding or restricting a food can make that food more desirable – out of sight is not out of mind when it comes to snacks.

A HEALTHY BREAKFAST, WITH FOODS THAT RELEASE ENERGY SLOWLY OVER THE MORNING, MAY IMPROVE CHILDREN'S MEMORY AND ATTENTION AT SCHOOL.

The idea that children have a sugar rush if they have too many sugary foods at a party is a myth.

4. HOW TO BE SEXY

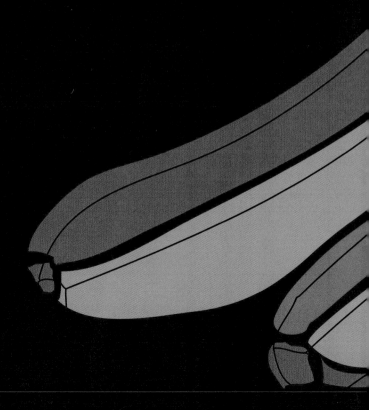

HOW TO BE SEXY

Food and sex: what a great combination. Food before sex, sex before food – or both at the same time, if that's how you like your whipped cream.

Apart from the sheer pleasure of combining food and sex, what you eat really can have a big influence on how good your sex life is. Take for example the ultimate purpose of all those candles and caresses: the sperm's journey through the cervix to the uterus, the fertilization of an egg, and nine months later the birth of another little miracle. To give this process the best chance of success, your body needs to be in great shape – and that means a healthy diet.

Unfortunately, there's a sperm crisis in the West at the moment and bad diet seems partly to blame. According to some studies, sperm counts have halved in the past fifty years, and the number of couples experiencing problems conceiving is doubling every ten years. On top of that, a lot of people are reporting a loss of libido – diminished desire. Combine the two problems and you've got fewer opportunities for fewer sperm.

We wanted to do our bit for those little guys, so in our main food-and-sex experiment for the television series we launched the Great Sperm Race. We took men with low sperm counts and changed their diets, then monitored their output over several months. As you'll see, the results were impressive.

There are lots of other ways food can improve your sex life – aphrodisiacs spring to mind. But do they really have any effect? One way to find out is to test the effect of food smells on the blood flow in a man's penis. We also investigated the possibility that garlic may be able to help if not enough blood is flowing to the penis.

For women, chocolate is the traditional sex drug. Women are said to like fatty, sweet foods, and chocolate is also supposed to contain compounds that get the sexual juices flowing. Men: on that third date, should you order the chocolate pudding even if you really want the cheese board, so she can eat half? Is chocolate really the love drug we think it is?

After you've got over the dating and desire stages,

there are foods that can make the actual event even better. Foods that make you taste better, where it counts. And there is evidence that foods might help make you a nicer person to have around as a partner, by reducing the symptoms of relationship-wrecking PMS – premenstrual syndrome.

Food and sex give pleasure and are essential to human life. You owe it to yourself to enjoy them both.

Culinary delight:
can foods turn you on?

The target of your affections is coming over for dinner in a couple of hours. Time to look over your seduction checklist: candles – in position; romantic music – lined up and ready to go; wine – champagne, of course, chilling in the fridge. But what are you going to make for dinner? What foods will get you both in the mood for love?

Well, why not start with oysters? As fresh and plump as you can get them, drizzled with white wine vinegar and glistening in the candlelight. (You've just got time to dash to the supermarket!) Then a rare tenderloin steak with a mustard sauce, rich and hot, and a green salad with avocado and pine nuts. Followed by raspberries and cream. And finally dark chocolates.

All of the foods above are traditional aphrodisiacs – believed to stimulate sexual desire. Yes, even the lettuce in the salad. You can add to the list licorice, honey, figs, truffles, bananas, basil, almonds – and, believe it or not, carrots. The idea is that your digestive juices won't be the only ones flowing.

Traditional these aphrodisiacs may be,

but do they work? Very little truly scientific research has been carried out into aphrodisiacs. Perhaps people prefer to retain the mystique surrounding these foods and not risk destroying it with science.

Passion killers

The US Food and Drug Administration (FDA) has no qualms about destroying the mystique of aphrodisiacs. In 1989, it declared that there was no proof that over-the-counter love potions boosted the libido. And since then, it has refused to endorse hundreds of food and drug products that make aphrodisiac claims.

And as if to kill any romantic ideas that might still remain, when it did finally give tentative credence to a libido-lifting substance in 2006, it wasn't a sweet, succulent or creamy food, or even a powder made from the genitals of a virile animal. It was bremelanotide – its name only slightly less unromantic than its experimental title, "PT-141." It comes as a colorless, odorless liquid that you inhale through a nasal spray.

But it really does seem to work – it is probably the first proven aphrodisiac. A final clinical trial of bremelanotide started in 2005 – involving men, though early trials have been conducted in women – and is likely to lead to FDA approval for marketing in a few years' time.

Bremelanotide was developed by a US pharmaceuticals company as a medicine to help people who suffer with sexual dysfunction or loss of libido (though it was originally tested as a sunless tanning agent). It works on women and men, and targets the brain, rather than blood flow as Viagra does. Several similar drugs are being developed. It looks as though the aphrodisiac industry will be a multi-billion-dollar money-maker. Eventually, the new generation of aphrodisiacs will probably find their way out into the mass market – just as Viagra did in 1998.

But wouldn't it be more romantic if we could fan the flames of desire with food? We'd still like to believe that the aphrodisiac foods of folklore might work. Some of the claims have been around for 4,000 years. How can they have had such an enduring reputation if they don't work?

That looks a bit like ...

Conventional scientific wisdom has it that many aphrodisiacs gained their reputation simply by association. For example, oysters are reminiscent of vulvas, while carrots, bananas and cucumbers have more than a passing resemblance to sturdy, erect penises. Similarly, "avocado" comes from an ancient Aztec word for "testicle." Virgin Aztec girls were banned from the fields during avocado harvesting time because of the provocative appearance of ripe fruits hanging from the branches of avocado trees.

Of course, explaining the effect of these foods as merely psychological doesn't completely rid them of their powers. The resemblance of food to genitalia could genuinely stir up desire, just not in the way the US Food and Drug Administration might demand before they can endorse a product. So if you are planning a seductive menu, serving bananas covered with cream might still be a good idea.

Psychology may also have a part to play when it comes to sex and hot or spicy foods. These foods can cause you to sweat and increase your heart rate, making you appear flushed. Again, by association, this could encourage you – and hopefully your partner – to feel a bit spicy, too.

Food does have a physical effect on the brain as well as a psychological effect on the mind. Both food and sex are essential for the survival of our species, so evolution has given our brains pleasure centres that "light up" in response to both sex and food.

When we eat and when we have sex, the brain produces lots of a chemical called dopamine in its pleasure centre. Tests show that dopamine is produced even at the sight of food. And, in several experiments with rats, researchers have blocked the action of dopamine with the result that the rats lost the desire both to eat and to have sex.

Sexual chemistry

But just because food and sex produce chemical pleasure in the same way inside the brain doesn't mean that food can encourage us to have sex, any more than having sex makes you want to eat.

A genuine aphrodisiac would do something different than simply stimulating the production of dopamine – it would do more than

make you feel good. It would heighten your desire, making you ready and willing for action. Are there any foods that affect your brain or your body in that kind of way?

Well, yes and no. One substance that you can eat that has a direct physical effect on your genitals is Spanish fly. It is an extract of an insect of the same name, and is perhaps the most notorious aphrodisiac. The active component of Spanish fly is an irritant called cantharidin. When you urinate, this chemical creates a burning sensation in your genitals, causing them to become inflamed. Not very romantic, but inflamed genitals are sensitive, excited genitals.

Spanish fly was once commonly used to encourage livestock to copulate, so it was only natural for people to try it. It is very toxic even in tiny amounts, and it can cause serious damage to your kidneys and blisters on your genitals. So it is best avoided, and is banned in many countries.

Another substance that has some claim to being a true aphrodisiac is yohimbine – also known as aphrodin. It is an extract of the bark of an African tree and is used to treat impotence. It has an effect on the brain – encouraging the production of adrenaline, which causes blood vessels to widen and the heart to race. It does have some unpleasant side effects if you exceed the correct dose – and it's not really a food. So the search goes on.

What about chocolate? It is often considered an aphrodisiac food – and not only because of its fatty, creamy, melt-in-the-mouth texture and its sweet taste. It contains a cocktail of chemicals that have an effect on the brain (see box). But opinions are divided as to what role these chemicals might have in arousal.

Of all the foods that people think of as aphrodisiacs, only oysters have any solid scientific evidence in their favor. It seems they might have more going for them than their looks.

Oysters have recently been found to contain the chemicals D-aspartic acid and NMDA. These act on the brain, encouraging the release elsewhere in the body of the sex hormones estrogen and testosterone. These slimy sea creatures also contain a lot of zinc, which is important in preserving male fertility – there is a lot of zinc in sperm. However, it is still not known whether oysters contain enough of these chemicals to make any real difference.

Sniff it out

The nose and genitals have something in common: they both contain erectile tissue, which swells as it engorges with blood before and during sex. There can be no confusion about why the penis needs to become erect, but for the vagina and the nose, it seems to be a case of increasing sensation. A nose pumped up with blood is much more sensitive to smells. And smell is a very important part of sex – nearly everyone who loses their sense of smell also loses much of their libido.

Most animals secrete subtle aromatic chemicals called pheromones, which act as chemical messengers. Some pheromones send messages of sexual availability. But the existence of human pheromones is still a matter of debate.

Could the aphrodisiac reputation of some foods simply be a result of their smells? Experimenters at the Smell and Taste Treatment and Research Center in Chicago say yes. In tests of sexual stimulation by smell alone, a combination of doughnuts and licorice increased blood flow to the penis by an average of 32 percent. Licorice and cucumber did it for the ladies, increasing vaginal blood flow by an average of 13 percent. We were intrigued.

Chocolate – the love drug?

More than 2,000 years ago, the Olmec people, who lived in part of what is now Mexico, discovered that you can make a mind-altering drink from the berries of a plant we call the cacao tree. The Aztecs, who lived nearby but hundreds of years later, associated that drink – chocolate – with their goddess of fertility. The Aztec emperor Montezuma II is said to have drunk fifty cups of chocolate a day in an attempt to maintain his sexual prowess. Solid chocolate was not widely available until 1847. But liquid or solid, can chocolate turn you on?

Chocolate is a very complex mixture of chemical compounds. Recently, researchers have discovered that it contains phenylethylamine – a "feel-good" chemical not unlike amphetamine (speed). In laboratory experiments, animals go crazy for this chemical, behaving as if they were engaged in courtship. But it seems to have less of an effect in humans. It can make you slightly more alert – but alert is not necessarily aroused.

Chocolate also contains tryptophan – an amino acid that produces another feel-good chemical, serotonin, inside the brain. Unfortunately, very little tryptophan from chocolate gets through to the brain, so it probably has no real effect.

The most intriguing compound in chocolate is anandamide – which gets its name from the Sanskrit word for "bliss." Anandamide is a neurotransmitter: a chemical involved in communication between brain cells. It targets the same areas of the brain as THC, the active component of cannabis. However, you would need to eat about 55 pounds of chocolate to get the same effect as a single joint.

Chocolate may not have any real aphrodisiac properties at all. But its melt-in-the-mouth texture makes it a very sensuous food. What woman wouldn't feel at least slightly aroused after receiving a romantic gift of chocolate?

The science test

In the first experiment of its kind ever, we compared the arousal effect of food aromas on men from different countries. Would different smells affect the penises of men from different cultures? Helping us in this bizarre experiment was Dr. Alan Hirsch, founder of the Smell and Taste Treatment and Research Center.

Dr. Hirsch came armed with a penile plethysmograph, and we met him at Santa Monica Beach, California. A plethysmograph is a device that accurately measures changes in volume of various body parts – it looks like a blood pressure monitor in miniature. On a penis, it can provide a good indication of sexual arousal. As our volunteers became excited, blood flow to their penises would increase and they would increase in size. But would that happen in response to the smells of foods? And if so, which ones?

We took nine men from the USA, three from the UK and three from Germany, and fitted each with a simple paper facemask. We measured a "baseline" penis size, when no aromas were present, and then dropped smelly liquids carrying food odors on to the mask so that the men inhaled the smells. Each man inhaled fifteen food scents chosen to represent favorite foods from each of the three different cultures. Would we see American men reacting more to pumpkin pie? The Germans going wild for sausage? Perhaps custard would cause blood to start pumping for the Brits.

What's up?

The table below shows the average increase in penis volume for the three nationalities. As you can see, men really do seem to be affected by different foods depending upon their culture. Perhaps a roast dinner should be served every Sunday in Germany, not in the UK.

Science test results

	BRITISH	AMERICAN	GERMAN
Pumpkin pie	16%	32%	8%
Orange	12%	6%	8%
Black licorice	4%	8%	12%
Cola	10%	14%	9%
Doughnuts	11%	17%	7%
Buttered popcorn	6%	14%	6%
Roast dinner	-4%	-1%	16%
Coffee	5%	-3%	10%
Vanilla	6%	15%	12%
Chocolate	3%	18%	3%
Fried potatoes	4%	-6%	14%
Apple cake	24%	12%	4%
Sausage	-3%	-10%	8%
Fish and chips	4 %	-18%	-6%
Custard	12%	5%	5%

The Great Sperm Race: eating for life

You're under pressure. You and your partner have been trying to make a baby for ages. It would make your lives complete. But so far, nothing. So here you stand – with a little plastic cup in your hand. What if your sperm count sample doesn't make the grade? How will you feel? How can you be expected to produce your best sample under this kind of pressure?

Despite the anxiety, you do eventually perform. But it's a temporary relief, because the anxiety isn't over yet. You have to get to the clinic, ideally within an hour, and hand the cup over to a nurse. And then you have to wait for the results.

More and more men are having to go through this ordeal now that the number of couples finding it difficult to conceive is on the increase. Statistics show that 40 percent of all cases are due to male infertility, with low sperm count the main underlying cause. The Western world could be heading for an infertility crisis.

We wanted to see whether changing men's diets could improve the quality of their semen. So we found five men who had already been diagnosed with low sperm counts and we set them a challenge: after six months of healthy eating, whose sperm would be the fittest? The Great Sperm Race was on.

Sperm count

Yes, sperm are very important. If a man and a woman want to conceive naturally, he'll need a healthy concentration of those little swimming marvels in his semen when he ejaculates.

Sure, it only takes one to fertilize an egg. But the more sperm there are, the better the chances. Many are lost along the way, and most of those that survive simply don't manage to get anywhere near the egg. And out of the millions of prospective sperm following chemical signals toward an egg, only the strongest will come anywhere close. It's success for the fittest – just another of nature's ways of ensuring the continuation of our species.

Sperm count is one of the most important factors in male fertility. The "normal" range is between 20 million and 300 million sperm cells per milliliter. That's more than a billion in each ejaculation at the top end of the scale. However, a thorough analysis of semen is as much to do with quality as quantity. Under the microscope, it is also possible to measure the "motility" of sperm – an estimate of how many are actually moving and how fast. It is also important to measure what proportion are not properly formed.

Several major studies have revealed a worrying trend in the USA and Europe. More and more men are producing semen with low sperm concentrations, and with decreased motility and an increased rate of malformation.

The average number of sperm per milliliter of semen has decreased in the past fifty years, from about 110 million to about 70 million. In 2005, a survey of UK doctors revealed that as many as 2.5 million men may be suffering from low fertility. There are several medical reasons why sperm counts might be low in particular individuals. But why should average sperm counts be on a downward slope?

Science fact: sperm factories

It takes about 70 days to make a mature sperm. Each sperm cell spends sixty days maturing inside the testicles – a process that includes growing a tail – and then spends another ten days or so traveling along the long, coiled tube called the epididymis. Just before ejaculation the mature sperm are mixed with semen, a fluid containing a complex mix of nutrients and other chemicals.

How come?

Most people assume that something about modern life is to blame for decreasing sperm counts. This makes sense when you consider one crucial difference between eggs and sperm. A woman is born with all the eggs she will ever have, just waiting their turn to mature, but men have to manufacture all their sperm from scratch.

So what environmental factors might be to blame for men's predicament? We have all heard reports of female hormones in the water supply, pesticides on our food and high levels of stress. All of these factors may play a part – although there is no conclusive evidence for any of them.

The temperature of a man's testicles certainly affects sperm count. Testicles are designed to dangle outside the body so they remain slightly cooler. Men who sit for long periods – such as long-distance drivers – and men who use laptops on their laps have unnaturally warm testicles and often dramatically reduced sperm counts.

Not surprisingly, heavy drinking and regular cannabis use have a detrimental effect on sperm count and motility, as can tobacco smoking, which also reduces blood flow to the penis, potentially leading to problems getting erections.

Research shows that diet is another factor. Vitamins, minerals and antioxidants are very important in producing enough healthy sperm. And it is these micronutrients that are lacking in many people's diets in the West.

Zinc is one mineral that plays a vital role in producing several components of semen, including the sperm themselves. You can find zinc in red meat, poultry, most breakfast cereals and shellfish – including oysters. Selenium is another important sperm-making mineral. Sources include butter, fish, garlic, Brazil nuts and sunflower seeds. There is evidence that a lack of selenium leads to poor sperm motility.

Several other micronutrients are important for making healthy sperm – including folic acid, and vitamins C and E. Again, some studies suggest links between levels of these compounds in men's diets and sperm counts. The message that emerges when you put all this together is that eating a healthy balanced diet will increase your chances of having healthy sperm.

In Europe and the US – the places where sperm counts seem to be on the steepest decline – most people's diets are far removed from nutritionists' guidelines. Only 18 percent of American men and 20 percent of British men eat the recommended five portions of fruits and vegetables each day. And diets, like sperm counts, have changed steadily over the past fifty years, largely as a result of increasing access to sugary, salty and processed foods.

Could switching to a healthy diet help men produce more sperm? It is a tantalizing possibility, given the heartache of so many couples failing to conceive.

The science test

While we were making our television series, we looked at studies that investigated the role of bad diet in declining sperm production. They had all concentrated on statistics across large numbers of men – no research had been carried out in which sperm count and sperm quality were measured before and after a change in diet. So that's what we decided to do.

Before we started our experiment in earnest, we decided to settle a question that someone had seen in a magazine: does the flavor of semen depend on what a man eats? With a simple test, we wanted to find out if the best way to a man's semen is through his stomach. This would be a dramatic way to show the potential for diet to affect the quality of semen.

The taste of things to come

It started out as a bit of fun, but experimenting with the flavor of semen was to prove quite thought-provoking. We knew that its basic metallic flavor is due to zinc, but would the more complex molecules responsible for flavors be able to make it into semen unchanged?

Three couples agreed to take part in our tasty experiment. All three were in stable, loving relationships. Before the experiment began, we asked the men to eat only bland food, and to abstain from alcohol, for three days. This "washout" period served to clear out the men's systems of strong flavors.

We checked our volunteers into six rooms in a boutique hotel on Hollywood Boulevard. The men had to stay apart from their partners, and no kissing or other close contact was allowed – otherwise, the partners might have had a sneak preview of food smells before the test. For two-and-a-half days, we put each man on a different strict diet, and the test took place on the third day. We called the three diets: "Hot and Spicy," "Fabulously Fishy" and "Fantastically Fruity and Fresh" – the names speak for themselves.

Back at the hotel, we sent our three volunteers to private rooms where they produced samples of semen in glass vials. A hotel waitress collected the samples, and delivered them, fresh and warm, to the corresponding partner – taking care not to get the samples mixed up. The partners were given a menu containing four items – "Massively Meaty" was added as a decoy. They tasted the samples, and guessed which diet their partner had been following. The results? Well, two out of the three partners guessed right.

Perhaps surprisingly, the diet that was not correctly identified was "Hot and Spicy."

According to two-thirds of our very small experimental sample, the saying "you are what you eat" is even true for semen. It made it seem all the more likely that diet and sperm count might be linked. And so, back to the main experiment.

The Great Sperm Race

Several scientific studies have hinted at the exciting possibility that diet can affect sperm count and quality. We found six couples that were having problems conceiving. Each couple had already consulted fertility experts, and in each case the reason why they were not conceiving seemed to be the man's low sperm count and low sperm quality. Each man had been producing fewer than 20 million sperms per milliliter. The couples were described as "subfertile," but none of the women appeared to have any problem with fertility. We wanted to see if we could help these couples, just by implementing a healthy diet.

The experiment ran for six months. At the outset, at four months and again at the end, the men had to provide samples of their semen. The samples were analyzed in detail by Dr. Allan Pacey, Senior Lecturer in Andrology (male reproductive health) at the University of Sheffield.

We called in nutritionist Fiona Ford, also based at the University of Sheffield. Fiona analyzed what each man was eating in a typical week, and identified which micronutrients vital for sperm creation were missing or in short supply. From this, she produced an individual set of recommendations. Each man drank one smoothie in the morning and another in the evening. The smoothie recipes were designed to address any lack of the following micronutrients that are thought to be important in sperm production: zinc, folate (from folic acid), selenium, omega-3 fatty acids, and a range of antioxidants including vitamin E, beta carotene and vitamin C.

Sperm characteristics

For each semen sample, Dr. Pacey carried out a range of standard tests, and worked out the following:

✳ the sperm concentration (millions per milliliter)

✳ the percentage of sperm that were moving

✳ concentration of moving sperm (millions per milliliter)

✳ percentage of sperm of normal size and shape (morphology)

✳ the total number of sperm ejaculated (millions)

✳ the total number of moving sperm ejaculated (millions)

Dr. Pacey also measured how well the sperm could "migrate" through a gel – an indication of how "healthy" they were.

Finally, he worked out the extent of DNA fragmentation – whether there were any errors in the DNA the sperm carried. The higher the percentage of damaged DNA, the less chance there is of producing a healthy baby.

The results

All six men provided sperm samples at the beginning of the study. When it came to the test at four months, two of the men could no longer be counted as part of the study. One dropped out after three months, for personal reasons.

Another man stopped the smoothie diet for a very different reason: his wife fell pregnant! Whether or not this was due to our intervention, we'll never know. So how did the remaining four men get on?

The six initial sperm counts ranged from just under a million sperms per milliliter up to just over the 20 million mark for two of the men. At the end of the experiment, the four men remaining showed no real change: two counts had gone up, two had gone down.

An interesting positive result was sperm morphology – a measure of how normal the sperms looked. We could only really make comparisons for the four men still in the study after four months. At the outset, the proportion of normal-looking sperm ranged from 0.5 percent to 10 percent. At the end, those figures had risen to between 1 and 12.5 percent. Importantly, every man showed an improvement – and three of them doubled their score.

An important factor that seemed to improve during our study was the state of the sperms' DNA. This is a major factor in making an embryo that has a good chance of going on to become a baby. When the experiment began, between 13 and 23 percent of the sperms carried DNA damage. By the time it finished, these figures had gone down to between 4 and 10 percent. Again, all four men showed an improvement. Overall, the results are encouraging.

The reduction in damage to the sperms' DNA is probably a result of the increased intake of antioxidants in the men's diets. The antioxidants "mop up" molecules called free radicals, which are known to damage DNA. Improvements in sperm morphology may be a direct result of the reduced damage to DNA.

Our study doesn't prove anything, but it does suggest that you can improve your chances of conceiving just by having a healthy diet. If you are having problems conceiving, and you're worried about your sperm count, there's no harm in trying the following regime: eat a healthy, balanced diet, reduce your stress levels, don't drink to excess, give up smoking if you are a smoker – and have lots of great sex.

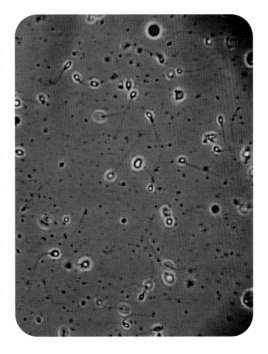

Diet really can affect sperm quality. We fed a group of "subfertile" men a tailor-made diet, with everything they needed to make healthy sperm. This photograph, taken through a microscope, shows sperms from the "winner" of the Great Sperm Race: his sperm quality improved the most. The proportion of normal sperms had doubled, to 5 percent; sperm with damaged DNA had halved, to 7 percent; sperm count had increased by 4 million per milliliter.

TOP TIPS – *The Truth About Food* Good Sperm Diet

* The quality of sperm can be affected by your diet and general health. In general, to maintain it you should:

* Eat a healthy diet, low in fat (particularly saturated fat), rich in unrefined carbohydrates, fruits and vegetables, with some low-fat dairy and lean meat. This way you'll ensure that you have all the right nutrients for health and healthy sperm.

* Maintain a healthy weight.

* Avoid drinking too much alcohol.

* In the experiment the volunteers boosted their intakes of selenium, folate and vitamins C, E and A. If you want to try the same diet, try the following:

* drink a couple of smoothies every day. Here are some examples, just blend for a minute and drink:

Very Berry
2 handfuls strawberries
2 handfuls raspberries
10 tablespoons (150ml) cranberry juice

Peachy Treat
1¹/₂ peaches
¹/₂ mango
¹/₂ orange
100ml orange juice

Papaya Pleasure
1 papaya
¹/₄ pineapple
50g black currants
120ml pineapple juice

The volunteers also included in their daily diet the following:

All these ingredients
65g (3 tablespoons) wheat germ
5–6 Brazil nuts
50g (1 medium) raw carrot

Two foods from this list:
20g (1) oyster
180g (medium can) of crab
140g quorn (pieces, mince/fillets, as purchased)
60g wheat bran
165g All-Bran

... and six of these:
5g (1 teaspoon) Marmite
50g black-eyed peas
50g low-fat soy flour
130g beetroot
60g spinach
80g asparagus
3 portions of spinach
and 3 of beans

There are several ways to include the foods in your diet:

1 Put the ingredients into your blender and include them in a smoothie
2 Eat some of them as they are
3 Incorporate them into your usual meals.

Garlic: nature's Viagra?

A strong erection is a key part of good sex for most people. Gossip about "not being able to get it up" might prompt sniggers, but it's no joke for the men involved – or their partners. You could turn to Viagra, but you might not need to. Amazingly, garlic might be able to fix the problem, or prevent it occurring at all.

Garlic has long been considered an aphrodisiac, in many different cultures. For example, the prophet Ezra instituted ten regulations to be followed by Jewish people. Among them was eating garlic on Fridays, which was said to "promote love and arouse desire."

We had heard that volunteers in some experiments with garlic reported improvements in their sex lives. We needed to check this out.

The wonder bulb

For thousands of years, garlic has been used to treat an enormous range of medical conditions. In *Natural History*, written 2,000 years ago, the Greek scholar Pliny the Elder describes sixty-one remedies involving garlic. They include boiled garlic for asthma; garlic in wine for snake bites; garlic mashed, mixed in vinegar and then gargled for tonsillitis; boiled garlic mixed with honey for blisters; and a strong garlic infusion rubbed on the temples for headaches. Pliny also mentions that garlic is an aphrodisiac – crushed with fresh coriander and mixed in wine.

Garlic breath

Most people find the smell of garlic on their lover's breath more of a turn-off than a turn-on. The strong aroma is due to compounds that contain sulfur – the very same compounds that give garlic many of its medicinal properties.

Parsley is a natural breath freshener and can even neutralize the strong aroma of garlic, which may be why many recipes that contain garlic also contain parsley. Other ways of ridding yourself of bad breath are: chew parsley, munch a coffee bean or chew a few anise or fennel seeds.

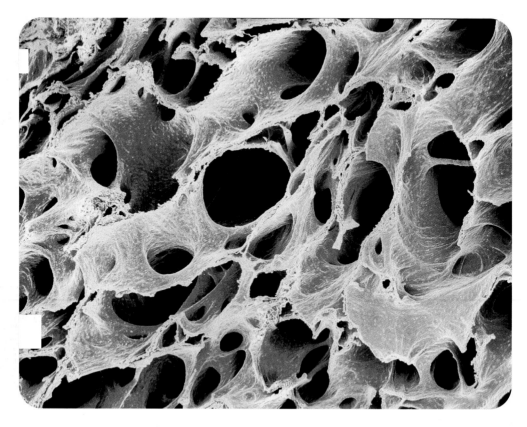

A penis becomes erect when blood fills spaces in sponge-like tissue running along its length. This picture, taken with a scanning electron microscope, shows the spaces in that tissue. The spongy tissue expands, and this helps to prevent the blood from leaving, by putting pressure on channels that lead back into the rest of body.

However whimsical these remedies might sound, some of them probably work. Similar remedies involving garlic are found in many other cultures and across many centuries. Garlic has the nickname "Russian penicillin," because Russian soldiers in both World Wars carried garlic cloves in their pockets to treat their wounds. Even today, practitioners of herbal medicine prescribe garlic for a range of ailments, including athlete's foot, dandruff and bronchitis.

Scientists began to take notice of garlic in 1858, when French biologist Louis Pasteur studied its antibacterial properties. In the past forty years, the list of health benefits recognized by science has grown significantly.

Garlic is loaded with nearly 100 active chemical compounds, including several potent antioxidants – compounds that reduce wear and tear on your body's cells. We don't yet fully understand how all of garlic's constituents work in the body, but garlic really does have antibiotic, decongestant, anti-cancer, anti-inflammatory, anti-fungal and even some anti-viral properties.

These amazing qualities are part of garlic's natural defense system, which is almost as well developed as our own. Scientific interest in garlic's medicinal qualities center on the sulfur-containing compounds it contains. The most important of these seems to be allicin, which forms when you crush or slice a garlic bulb and is the plant's natural weapon against bacterial and fungal attack.

And there's more. Since the 1970s, science has given credence to something your grandmother might have said: garlic is good for the blood. Several long-term studies and individual experiments have shown almost conclusively that it lowers blood cholesterol – accepted by most doctors as a major factor in heart disease. One long-term study in Europe, in 1992, compared a concentrated preparation made from garlic extract with one of the best anti-cholesterol drugs. There was little to choose between the two treatments. Garlic also makes the blood flow a bit more freely, by making the disc-shaped platelets, responsible for clotting, clump together less. Several studies also suggest that it can lower your blood pressure. It is garlic's effect on the blood that could put the oomph back into your sex life.

science jargon buster

Warding off bad cholesterol

Several studies have been carried out into the effect of garlic on blood cholesterol level. Increased levels of "bad cholesterol" (low-density lipoprotein or LDL) are blamed for the hardening of arteries – the buildup of "plaque" on their lining that is the main cause of heart disease.

Most of the research suggests that garlic reduces blood cholesterol, and studies in mice have shown that allicin, its main active component, reduces the buildup of plaque. Studies involving people have even shown the level of plaque formation, which normally increases with age, leveling off and even regressing after garlic therapy.

science jargon buster

Allicin Wonderland

The most important chemical in garlic seems to be allicin. Recent research has highlighted its potential in preventing or treating cancers, malaria and tuberculosis. Allicin even shows promise as a weapon against the "hospital superbug" MRSA (methicillin-resistant Staphylococcus aureus), which is unaffected by most antibiotics.

Allicin is an unstable compound – in other words, it breaks down into other chemicals very easily. Inside the body, it is probably these "daughter" chemicals that do the good work.

Things are looking up

What happens when a man gets an erection? The main body of the penis is made up of elastic connective tissue and spaces for blood to flow into, all surrounded by muscle. When a man is sexually aroused, blood flows in to fill up the empty spaces, enlarging and elevating the penis. When those spaces are filled, they act like a one-way valve, compressing the veins so blood cannot flow back out. This keeps the penis hard.

Needless to say, sometimes the penis doesn't behave as it is supposed to. An estimated 2 million men in the UK, and around 20 million in the USA, suffer from impotence or "erectile dysfunction." The problem increases with age: almost 90 percent of men over seventy experience it to some degree.

Trouble getting an erection or maintaining it used to be attributed to purely psychological factors. These certainly can play a part – lack of confidence or declining libido does lead to erectile dysfunction. But physiological causes are often to blame. Diabetes is one potential cause, for example, probably because the condition can damage nerves in the penis, making it less sensitive.

But given the role of blood in creating and sustaining an erection, blood health is usually the most important factor. The fact that people today lead less active lives and eat more fatty foods, which can increase blood cholesterol, could go some way to explaining why erectile dysfunction is on the increase.

One approach to tackling erectile dysfunction is to increase the potency of a chemical in the body called nitric oxide. That is how Viagra works. Nitric oxide plays a key role in erections: it relaxes muscle tissue in the walls of blood vessels in the penis. This opens up the vessels and increases the flow of blood into it.

Amazingly, garlic encourages your body to produce more nitric oxide. By reducing cholesterol and improving blood flow, it also boosts your blood's health in general, which Viagra doesn't. There is even growing evidence that regular intake of garlic can help to improve some kinds of diabetes.

In previous published studies examining the effect of garlic on the blood, some men had reported improved erectile function. We wanted to follow up that finding. For the television program, we placed seven men on a diet and exercise regime that included a daily intake of garlic. It was the first study to look at the possible use of garlic to treat erectile dysfunction. The results were impressive: six of the seven men reported improved erections.

No one yet knows for sure if garlic has a similar effect to Viagra. But there's certainly no harm in including lots of it in your diet – whether you suffer from erectile dysfunction or not.

TOP TIPS – Getting the best from garlic

If you want to make the most of the effects of allicin in garlic, follow these tips:

* Eat at least three cloves of garlic every day
* Raw garlic is best
* Chop it or crush it to trigger the enzyme reaction that creates allicin
* If cooked, then for a very brief period of time – no longer than 10 minutes

Which garlic is best?

Analysis in the lab of five different garlic strains showed that the amount of active ingredient allicin varied greatly between them. The strain that came out on top is Spanish Morado, the garlic found on most supermarket shelves – the familiar small white bulb most of us buy.

And remember: you can use parsley to help counteract the smell of garlic.

TRUTH ABOUT FOOD NO. 7:

THE AROMAS OF FOOD CAN AFFECT THE VOLUME OF BLOOD FLOWING INTO A MAN'S PENIS.

GARLIC CAUSES THE BODY TO RELEASE NITRIC OXIDE INTO THE BLOODSTREAM. SO DOES VIAGRA.

Dinner date:
eat less to impress?

Most men need all the help they can get to read the subtle signs of romance. Well here's a tip: if you're out for a meal for a first time with a woman, watch how she eats – or rather, how much she eats.

If your date leaves half her food, it could mean that looking at you makes her so sick she can't eat. Alternatively, it might mean quite the opposite: that she is keen for you to perceive her as feminine because she likes you.

Most of us – women and men – assume that slim equals desirable, and that "ladies" eat in a ladylike fashion. An old experiment from the 1980s suggested this was the case, so we thought we'd better try it out. On two different dates in the same swanky restaurant, we watched how much women ate when accompanied by men with very different prospects.

Sweet nothings

Flirting is innate: it's in your genes. Men and women are programed to hunt for a mate –

someone who will help them pass on their genes. And we would rather have a healthy partner – to maximize the chance that our offspring, and therefore our genes, will survive. Some of it is verbal, some of it is body language. But when we see a potential match, the way we behave – either consciously or unconsciously – tells them that we would like to have sex with them.

There are all sorts of things we look for in a perfect mate. For example, studies have shown that we find faces and bodies attractive if they are symmetrical. This ties in nicely with other research showing that the most symmetrical people are the ones with the "fittest" genes. Smell is another important factor. Experiments show that the people whose smell we find most attractive have combinations of genes that would work well with our own. Your nose is a genetic testing device.

Another feature men tend to look for is the ratio of waist to hips. Men find women most attractive if the circumference of their waist is 70 percent the circumference of their hips. Women with this body shape – Marilyn Monroe is a good example – are perceived as having "child-bearing hips."

Our perception of genetic fitness – through things like smell and symmetry – is universal, unchanging and deep-seated. But we also assess potential mates on cultural factors, which can change through time and vary from place to place.

Ever wondered why women are generally more concerned about their weight than men are? A big part of the reason is that we tend to equate thinness in women with attractiveness and success – in the West, in modern times, at least.

In some other cultures there is less emphasis on being thin; and hundreds of years ago in Europe, the emphasis was different, too. If you were powerful and successful, you would have had more access to food and would be more likely to be large. That's why the scantily clad women reclining on velvet chaises longues in Renaissance paintings were so well-upholstered. Back then everyone thought buxom was beautiful.

Today, glossy magazines are filled with images of thinness. We tend to assume that thin women are more likely to achieve status and be popular, and to have the best chance of catching themselves a fit, successful man. As a result, do we also make assumptions about the way desirable women should eat?

The science test

In several experiments in the 1980s and 1990s, psychologists showed that men find women more feminine if they are light eaters than if they munch their way through huge platefuls of food.

Women: if you were with someone you saw as a potential mate, surely you would want him to see you as feminine?

So the theory goes that women pick at their food if they are sitting opposite a hot prospect, and eat like there's no tomorrow if they are with someone less desirable. Does this play out in practice? A 1987 study, carried out by Shelley Chaiken and Patricia Pliner, at Vanderbilt University, Tennessee, suggested that it did. But a similar study, also carried out by (now Professor) Pliner, and published in 2004, seems to contradict it. In the more recent experiment, men found the big eaters more attractive. We decided to see if we could settle the question.

We carried out our experiment in the swanky restaurant of the National Gallery in central London. We based our test on the 1987 study, which was done in the USA with young American college students.

Our chosen women knew they were taking part in a BBC program about dating, but we didn't tell them exactly what was going on. After recruiting the women we had to find men who could play the roles of desirable and not-so-desirable dinner dates.

Psychologists have looked into what factors make men most attractive to women. You can see profiles of "Mr. Desirable" and "Mr. Undesirable" in the box.

Armed with our list of characteristics, we found some men who could be Mr. Desirable and Mr. Undesirable. We asked the women exactly what they like in a man, and then told the Mr. Desirable men to pretend they liked the same things. Mr. Undesirable had to pretend to have no hobbies, no interest in current affairs, no sense of humor and to have an unimportant and less-well-paid job.

The experiment was carried out in two stages. The first date was with Mr. Desirable, the second, later in the week, was with Mr. Undesirable. The food was the same on both dates, and the kitchen staff at the restaurant weighed the food they sent out and weighed the leftovers.

According to psychologists, and pooled from many different surveys, Mr. Desirable ...

* is interested in traveling, cooking, photography, reading and participating in sports;
* is unattached, has never divorced and has no children from previous partners;
* is professional and high-earning;
* is good-looking, symmetrical; tall; good dress sense; not smelly; clean teeth;
* is two to four years older than the woman;
* is cleverer than the woman, with a good sense of humor;
* reads widely and keeps abreast of the news;
* demonstrates a caring disposition.

Mr. Undesirable ...

* has no hobbies apart from watching television, drinking and gambling;
* has children with previous partners;
* does an unimportant, less well-paid job;
* is younger than the woman;
* reads tabloid newspapers and has no interest in current affairs;
* has no sense of humor.

The results

Our experimental results did not support the theory that women eat less when they are dining with someone they fancy. Even though they all confirmed that they really were more attracted to the Mr. Desirables than to the Mr. Undesirables, only one of the five women actually ate less on the first date with the man they fancied.

It seems that attitudes have changed since 1987 and our result tied in with a 2004 study. Twenty-first-century men prefer normal weight women who eat heartily. This is probably because over the last twenty years there has been a backlash against dieting which has put the focus on eating healthily and maintaining body weight, rather than dieting. Nowadays more people recognize that it is better to eat heartily and healthily.

So it's good news for women. If you get taken out for a delicious meal by the man of your dreams, eat up, he'll fancy you more if you eat well and don't just pick at a few lettuce leaves.

But it's bad news for men. You're going to have to rely on other body signs to find out if she fancies you or not.

PMS:
the Double-D diet

Oh joy! It's that time again. A week or so before your period, and here are the headaches, the swollen ankles, tender breasts and worst of all, horrible mood swings – all the way from "pissed off" to "extremely pissed off." And then there's the anxiety and that uncontrollable desire to lash out. These are the symptoms of premenstrual syndrome (PMS), and they will sound horribly familiar to many women.

About three-quarters of all women will suffer from PMS at some time in their lives. A third of women suffer enough to have their everyday lives disrupted for a few days each month. And about 5 percent of women suffer so badly they have a different name for their condition: premenstrual dysphoric disorder. The name is suitably gruesome – this condition is so much more than just a monthly bad mood.

Don't take it out on me

According to some men, PMS is all in the mind. The body's going through a bit of a change before you have your period, they tell their partners, so it's only natural you'll feel a little bit strange. It's not like you don't know it's going to happen. You've had enough practice – just pull yourself together. But whatever you do, don't take it out on me.

Warning! This kind of "expert" analysis can push an already stressed-out brain into anger overload.

So what does cause PMS? Some researchers believe it is caused by – or at least exacerbated by – social factors. In particular, people who support this idea suggest that unsympathetic male partners have a great deal to answer for. In 2005, an Australian researcher found that single women and those in same-sex relationships tended to suffer less from PMS than those in heterosexual relationships.

While psychological factors such as a lack of sympathy from those around you might play a part in PMS, they really can't be the root cause of such a debilitating and unwelcome disruption of your body and mind. And while a bit of sympathy might make the symptoms of PMS a little bit easier to deal with, it won't make them disappear.

There must be something biological behind PMS. And the obvious place to start is hormones.

You're imbalanced

How many times have you heard women say, "Sorry: it's my hormones." Just before menstruation, there are big changes in the concentrations of the female hormones estrogen and progesterone in the bloodstream. Estrogen levels fall, while progesterone levels increase. These two hormones are produced in the ovaries, and when women have their ovaries removed, PMS always disappears.

But there must be more to it than hormones because women who don't suffer from PMS have the same changes in hormone concentration as those who do. Perhaps the brains of PMS sufferers are different in some way – more sensitive to progesterone, for example.

There are a few subtle chemical differences between the brains of PMS sufferers and non-sufferers. In particular, sufferers have lower levels of an important chemical messenger called serotonin, which is important in determining your mood. Doctors sometimes prescribe drugs that help maintain or increase the level of serotonin – including Prozac – and these drugs are often effective. Chocolate increases serotonin levels slightly. Imagine that: eating chocolate to cure PMS. It's many women's idea of heaven. Sadly, chocolate doesn't seem to have the same power as Prozac against PMS. Herbal remedies such as St.-John's-wort and evening primrose oil seem to work for some people, but conclusive evidence is still lacking.

Most women would prefer to alleviate their PMS symptoms by changing their diet rather than by taking antidepressants or having their ovaries removed. So, can what you eat really affect PMS?

Diet and PMS

There is plenty of evidence that diet plays a part in PMS. The standard medical treatment for the condition begins with simple changes in lifestyle. At least, they are simple in theory, but maybe not so easy to achieve in practice: reduce caffeine, alcohol and salt intake. Relaxation and stress-avoidance are also prescribed.

Blood-sugar level also seems to be important. Some women with PMS report having cravings for sugary foods between ovulation and menstruation, but unfortunately treats like these have a high glycemic index (GI). This means they release glucose into the bloodstream rapidly. Research suggests that if you want to improve your mood by boosting serotonin levels, low-GI carbohydrates are best – that's starchy, high-fiber foods like brown rice, whole grain bread, spaghetti and noodles.

Vitamins and minerals also seem to play an important role. In particular, vitamin B6 is involved in your body's production of serotonin. You can find this vitamin in fish, chicken, green beans, bananas and wheat germ. Research showing that the availability of vitamin B6 in the body is reduced in PMS sufferers has prompted some women to take vitamin B6 supplements. However, there is no convincing evidence that it actually makes any difference. And it is easy to take too much – overloading on B6 can cause nerve damage.

The big news in PMS research at the moment concerns a clever combination of a mineral and a vitamin: calcium with vitamin D. Calcium is vital – not just for building healthy teeth and bones, but also in a huge number of other vital body processes. Researchers have shown that calcium supplements (taken with vitamin D supplements) can reduce the severity of PMS symptoms by half, in just under 50 percent of sufferers.

Vitamin D fulfills many vital roles, too – the most important being to help your body absorb calcium from food. You can see why they make such a great partnership. If you have low levels of vitamin D, nearly all the calcium in your food will pass straight through. So, if calcium is an effective weapon against PMS, then vitamin D is just as important.

The science test

An exciting new approach to combating the annoying phenomenon of PMS uses a combination of vitamin D and calcium. A few studies have been done, but none so far have used food. So with the help of Nigel Denby, Senior Dietician at Hammersmith Hospital and Queen Charlotte's Menopause and Women's Health clinic, London, we devised the "Double-D" anti-PMS diet. D is for dairy – a good source of calcium; and D is for vitamin D, which is essential if the calcium is to be absorbed.

The Double-D diet can be used as an add-on to what you normally eat: a controlled extra calcium intake from dairy foods, and extra vitamin D from boiled eggs and fortified margarine. You can also manufacture your own vitamin D if you go out in the midday sunshine. We chose not to include sunbathing in our diet plan, because of the risks of overdoing it – and because it would never have been a reliable part of the experiment.

We called on Dr. Nick Panay, a leading expert on PMS, for help with medical diagnosis. Dr. Panay found fifteen sufferers, and we divided them into two groups: half the women followed the Double-D diet, the others continued as normal.

The results were impressive. The women who followed the Double-D diet had a better than one-third improvement in their scores in depression and mood swing tests. The other women showed no significant improvement. Our experiment was small, but it suggests that increasing your calcium and vitamin D intake really can make a difference. If you suffer from horrible moods every month, why not try it – the details are in the Top Tips box.

Vitamin D – the sunshine vitamin

The main function of vitamin D in the body is to help absorb calcium. But studies also suggest that having enough vitamin D can protect against colon, breast and ovarian cancers.

The biggest source of vitamin D is sunshine. This important vitamin is produced inside your skin when ultraviolet radiation in sunlight hits your body. But it only happens when the sun is quite high in the sky – only for an hour or two each day in summer, and in many countries not at all during the winter. The main consequences of vitamin D deficiency are rickets and osteoporosis. If you have dark skin you are at particular risk, because the pigment in your skin blocks the ultraviolet radiation.

Not many foods naturally contain vitamin D: oily fish, beef liver and, to a lesser extent, eggs, milk and cereals. Many foods are artificially fortified with vitamin D, including some margarines, breakfast cereals and soy milk.

TOP TIPS – Double-D diet

If you want to try the same diet the women did in the experiment, then every day you should consume:

✳ 1,500 milligrams (mg) of calcium*

✳ 20 micrograms (μg) of vitamin D

Sources of calcium

300ml semi-skimmed milk – 360mg calcium

300ml semi-skimmed milk with additional 50g dried skim milk powder – 1,000mg

150g cup of low-fat yogurt – 285mg

75g cheddar cheese – 540mg

75g reduced-fat cheddar cheese – 630mg

75g Parmesan cheese – 900mg

75g Edam cheese – 578mg

Vitamin D:

There are not many foods which contain a lot of vitamin D, but the list below are the best sources.

100g grilled herring – 25μg vitamin D

100g baked kipper – 25μg

100g smoked mackerel – 8μg

100g canned salmon – 12.5μg

100g sardines in tomato sauce – 7.5μg

These examples of oily fish are clearly the richest sources of vitamin D from food. However, in certain circumstances, it is not recommended to eat oily fish every day. If you are planning a pregnancy or could become pregnant you must only eat three 100g portions of oily fish each week. You should also avoid eating shark, swordfish and marlin, and limit tuna steaks to no more than two per week.

The following foods also contain vitamin D

50g low-fat spread – 2μg

100g tuna in oil (drained) – 5.8μg

70g boiled egg (large) – 1.2μg

100g plain omelette (made with 2 eggs) – 1.6μg

100g flapjack made with soft margarine – 2.3μg

Check the labels on breakfast cereals – some of them are fortified with vitamin D.

---

*If you intend to take supplements, rather than obtaining your calcium and vitamin D from food, you should be aware that the "Expert Report on Vitamins and Mineral Supplements" recommends that calcium supplements should not exceed 1,500mg per day and vitamin D, 25 μg per day.

SUMMARY:
HOW TO BE SEXY

OF THE MANY EVERYDAY FOODS THAT WE THINK OF AS APHRODISIACS, PROBABLY VERY FEW HAVE ANY REAL EFFECT ... BUT SMELL IS POWERFUL, AND FOOD AROMAS CAN TURN YOU ON.

Evidence suggests that sperm counts and sperm quality have reduced dramatically over the past fifty years; a healthy diet can help to improve sperm quality.

GARLIC HAS SOME AMAZING EFFECTS ON THE BLOOD VESSELS, REDUCING THE LIKELIHOOD OF STROKE AND HEART DISEASE; THOSE EFFECTS COULD MEAN THAT A DIET RICH IN GARLIC CAN HELP MEN OVERCOME ERECTILE DYSFUNCTION.

 There is evidence that men fancy women more who eat heartily, although thirty years ago, they tended to fancy women who ate less.

 CALCIUM HAS BEEN SHOWN TO BE EFFECTIVE IN REDUCING THE HORRIBLE EFFECTS OF PREMENSTRUAL SYNDROME (PMS); VITAMIN D IS IMPORTANT, TOO, SINCE IT HELPS THE BODY ABSORB CALCIUM.

5. HOW TO BE THE BEST

HOW TO BE THE BEST

Our culture celebrates winners, champions, coming out on top, being number one. Think Roger Federer, Jackie Joyner-Kersee, Carl Lewis, Bill Gates, Madonna ...

Being the best is what matters in sports and entertainment, and apparently it does in the workplace, too. TV dramas and ad breaks show us offices populated with hard-driving executives, tanned and toned, focused, dressed to kill, high-energy overachievers. If you can't keep up with them on that treadmill you're on the downward spiral of a loser.

Fortunately there's a lot more to life than coming out on top. But aren't there times when you wish you had, well, a little extra "oomph"?

Becoming a winner is sometimes about pure talent, but usually talent only plays a small part. It's mainly about energy and tenacity. It's about being fastest off the blocks, then running longer and harder than the rest of the field. We know we could all be winners if only we could muster a big enough burst of energy at the right moment, or build up our stamina for the long run – like those old adverts where the toy bunny packing the longer-life batteries just keeps on going.

But we ordinary mortals struggle every day to wake ourselves up, to kick-start our brains and bodies, to get focused. And every few hours there's that sense of dulling and slowing down, the need for the quick nap to recharge, the loss of edge and attention. Food really can make a difference, providing energy for the short run and the long run, for optimum physical and mental performance. With the right kind of food you can be the best.

Let's start by looking at that tired old body. For the TV program on fitness we looked at whether meat can boost muscle performance. We got a team of vegetarian martial arts enthusiasts to become meat-eaters for a whole month. Then we looked at how eating patterns affect stamina and energy levels. Specifically, whether you should eat smaller meals more frequently, when you're hungry, or whether you should follow the traditional three-big-meals-a-day pattern. We got a bunch of wildfire fighters to help us out.

To provide a short and sharp energy boost, most of us would go for something with plenty of sugar, glucose or other carbohydrates. We looked at the additional kick you can get by combining caffeine with an intake of carbohydrate.

Then let's investigate that slow old brain. Staying with caffeine, we looked at the science underlying caffeine's ability to stimulate short-term brain performance. In terms of long-term brainpower, omega-3 fatty acid seems to have wonderfully positive effects, and eating oily fish is the best way to get it. Not only does it enhance brain performance, it also seems to help the brain cope better with stress. We got a group of London cabbies to consume regular doses of omega-3 in oily fish for three months to see what it would do for them.

And returning to carbohydrates and performance, we found that mind counts as much as matter. Carbohydrates are so important that we have evolved a way to kick-start the body at the merest whiff of them. Finally, we investigated the science behind something that causes you to perform well below par: the hangover.

Meat-free:
does it mean muscle-free?

Most people assume that eating plenty of meat is the best way to build up your muscles. So if you're a vegetarian, you must be at a distinct disadvantage.

To find out if this is true, we asked veggie volunteers to abandon their meat-free diet for four weeks. We tested their strength and endurance before and afterward. Our brave veggies weren't track-and-field athletes or body-builders. They were dedicated followers of martial arts.

Veggie views

The martial arts have a long association with vegetarianism: many of the founders of the various disciplines were Buddhist monks who were vegetarian for spiritual reasons. Today, there are several motivations other than spiritual ones why people choose not to eat meat.

For many, vegetarianism is an animal-rights issue. Others object to meat production because it is very inefficient in terms of water and energy. For example, an acre of land given over to growing crops typically produces ten times the energy and protein as the same acre used to feed meat-producing livestock.

Then there are people who choose a vegetarian diet for their health. Fruits, nuts, pulses and vegetables provide dietary fiber, proteins, vitamins and minerals. They are low in fat and most of the fats that they do contain are unsaturated (although nuts contain saturated fats). Evidence suggests that unsaturated fats are healthier than the saturated fats, common in most meat. Fruits and vegetables also provide a wealth of antioxidants: chemicals that can help to prevent damage within your body's cells. Vegetarians tend to have lower rates of heart disease, obesity, diabetes and most forms of cancer.

Despite the benefits, vegetarians are relatively rare in the West. Only about one in twenty people in the UK and the USA is an ovo-lacto vegetarian: a vegetarian who eats eggs and dairy produce. And only about one in a hundred is vegan – eating no animal products

Vegetarians and vegans take care

Strict vegetarians need to be a little careful to ensure they get all the essential nutrients from their diets. Contrary to popular belief, protein is not a problem: even without eating eggs or dairy products, it is easy to get all the protein you need by having a balanced diet.

There is, however, an issue with vitamin B12. This compound is essential in several bodily processes, including making red blood cells. A B12 deficiency can lead to anemia, but fortunately we only need tiny amounts. There is plenty of vitamin B12 in eggs and dairy produce, so ovo-lacto vegetarians have no problems. Vegans can eat food fortified with B12, such as yeast extract.

Iron can be another area of concern – especially for teenaged and pregnant vegetarians. Iron from meat and fish is more easily absorbed by the body than iron from vegetable sources. Vitamin C, from citrus fruits for example, helps the body to absorb iron from vegetables (and eggs).

Finally, calcium can be an issue for vegans (ovo-lacto vegetarians can get all they need from dairy products). There are many non-dairy sources of calcium, although certain compounds in vegetables can inhibit the absorption of calcium. Again, variety is key.

---

whatsoever. Perhaps people simply like the taste and texture of meat.

But maybe there is more to it: most meat is largely made of muscle, which contains lots of protein and iron. Protein is essential for building up muscle fibers, and iron is the central element in hemoglobin, the oxygen-carrying molecule in red blood cells. The leanest meat is more or less pure muscle. So you would expect eating meat to make you feel strong and fit.

Feeding your muscles

The link between eating animals' muscles and building up our own is more than just psychological – and about more than just protein and iron. Eating meat supplies us with two chemical compounds that are important in muscle function,

creatine and carnosine, which are not present in vegetables.

If you are a keen bodybuilder, you will almost certainly have heard of creatine. In the 1990s it became popular as a muscle-building supplement, available in capsules and in powder form. Creatine occurs naturally in the body: its role is to help supply energy to your muscles.

Your muscles store creatine – and the more they have, the better they can perform. The stored creatine is all used up about ten seconds into intense exercise, but it can be recycled inside the muscles during a brief recovery period. So creatine is very important for explosive activity like punching and kicking. This substance is also important in the supply of energy in brain cells – and probably plays a role in quick reactions, important in many sports. Your liver, kid-

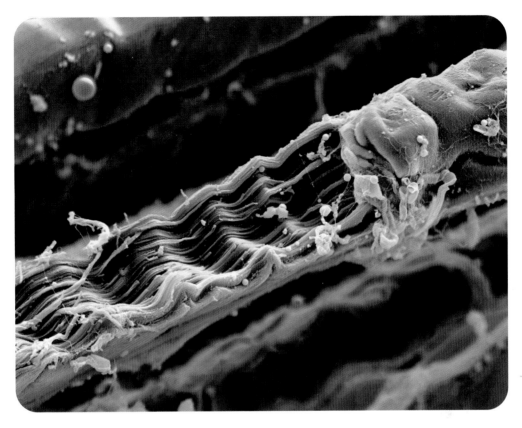

Muscles are made of bundles of fibers (red) held together by connective tissue (yellow). Each fiber is a very long living cell. In the foreground of this scanning electron micrograph is one fiber that has been cut open to reveal striped bands of two different proteins within the fiber. These proteins slide over each other when they receive nerve signals, making the muscle contract.

neys and pancreas manufacture creatine, so you're never without it.

Creatine is stored in other animals' muscles, too; if you are a meat-eater, you take some into your body when you eat meat or fish. And research shows that some of the creatine you take into your body – whether in your food or as supplements – really does add to your muscles' store of this important compound. So meat-eaters may be able to push their muscles a little further because they have extra creatine.

The other chemical, carnosine, has been dubbed the "new creatine." Like its prede-

cessor, carnosine is produced naturally inside your body and is stored in your muscles. It helps to reduce muscle fatigue and improves stamina. The more carnosine present, the longer and harder your muscles can work.

Carnosine is often marketed as an anti-aging product. This is because it is a powerful antioxidant, preventing the damage within your cells that seems to be the main cause of aging. It also helps to prevent glycation, a reaction between sugars and proteins that harms body tissues.

Vegetarians – and vegans – have no

TOP TIPS – Iron

Poor iron intakes have a negative effect on performance – we have less energy and tire easily. Women (aged 11–50 years) need 14.8mg (milligrams) of iron a day, men need 8.7mg.

Iron from animal sources is absorbed best.

		Vegetarians need to work to get enough iron:	
1 portion black pudding (75g)	15.0mg	120g cooked lentils (3 tbsp)	4.2mg
2 slices liver (100g)	9.0mg	12 ready-to-eat dried apricots	3.4mg
1 whole pig's kidney	9.0mg	8-oz can baked beans in tomato sauce	3.2mg
6 mollusks	6.2mg	2 slices whole wheat bread	1.9mg
225g lean beef steak	6.0mg	Pasta, cooked average portion (7½ tbsp)	1.8mg
1 chicken quarter	2.0mg	25g cashew nuts	1.6mg
1 medium egg	1.1mg	Large portion peas	1.4mg
1 small can tuna in brine	1.0mg	2 slices white bread	1.0mg
1 chicken breast	0.65mg	2 tbsp raisins	0.8mg
1 large fillet white fish	0.5mg	Large portion cabbage	0.7mg

Many breakfast cereals are enriched with iron.

To boost your iron intake:

Include a glass of orange or grapefruit juice with your daily breakfast cereal. Vitamin C helps the absorption of iron.

Don't drink tea and coffee with meals. Tannins in these drinks reduce the amount of iron absorbed.

Whole grain breads and cereals are better than those with added bran.

Creatine

You get about 1g of creatine per day by eating meat or fish in your diet. Strict vegetarians get negligible amounts from their diet. We all make about 1g per day in the kidney, liver and pancreas, whether we eat meat or not.

Food	Creatine content per 100g
Herring	0.65
Beef	0.45
Salmon	0.45
Pork	0.4
Tuna	0.4
Cod	0.3
Flounder	0.2
Milk	0.01
Cranberries	0.002

Cooking seems to destroy some of the creatine, so keep cooking time short (but long enough to make the food safe). Making casseroles and eating the gravy, or using meat juices to make gravy would help to minimize creatine losses.

problem getting all the "macronutrients" they need: carbohydrates, fats and proteins. But they may be missing out on some "micronutrients": any other useful chemicals in food that are needed in smaller amounts. Iron, creatine and carnosine can be in short supply or missing in some veggie diets. Might a lack of these micronutrients reduce vegetarians' performance? We wanted to find out.

Anaerobic respiration

Most of the time muscles get their energy when oxygen combines with glucose. This is called aerobic respiration. But during very strenuous or prolonged exercise, the supply of oxygen cannot keep up with demand. Under these conditions, the muscle turns to anaerobic respiration.

The downside to anaerobic respiration is that it results in a buildup of lactic acid in the muscle tissue, which in turn leads to pain and contributes to fatigue. Creatine helps your body to supply energy more efficiently in aerobic respiration, postponing the need for the muscle to use anaerobic respiration. And carnosine helps slow down the buildup of lactic acid.

The science test

Can switching to a meaty diet boost vegetarians' physical performance? We found twelve vegetarian and vegan women from around the country – each one practices either karate, judo or kickboxing. In all these disciplines, muscle power and quick reactions are essential. We worked with a team of scientists at the University of Chichester, headed by Glenys Jones. She is no stranger to studies about meat, and carnosine in particular. In previous research, she discovered that the best food you can eat to increase the production of carnosine in your own muscles is turkey breast.

Our experiment ran for three months. We made sure that none of our volunteers was taking creatine or carnosine supplements during this period – that would have ruined our experiment. We split our veggie volunteers into two groups, which we called "The Meat-eaters" and "The Vegetarians."

At the outset, we asked all our volunteers to undertake physical tests of strength, speed and stamina. There was a running task, which involved slowly increasing the speed of a treadmill and measuring how long it was before the participants asked us to stop the machine. There was also a leg strength test, in which the participants had to bend their knees backward and forward repeatedly in a machine that could measure the power of their leg muscles. We worked out the average force over the first three contractions, and over a total of thirty. Another test found out how long the participants could keep their balance, using a device called a Stabilometer.

Our volunteers also took mental tests of memory and reaction time. And finally, we took blood samples, so that we could measure the volunteers' iron levels.

The Meat-eaters then had to eat meat at least twice a day for three months, while The Vegetarians continued with their meat-free diets, which in some cases included eggs and dairy products, but no meat or fish. All the participants kept food diaries, and from this, we worked out that The Meat-eaters increased their intake of iron and vitamin B12 significantly.

At the end of the three months, our volunteers took the same tests again. The results were mixed, and were complicated by several factors. For example, before the first set of tests, one of our volunteers was ill, and one had drunk quite a lot of alcohol the night before. One of the participants suffered an ankle injury shortly before the second set of tests. In some of the tests, The Vegetarians actually improved more than The Meat-eaters, even though they hadn't changed their diets.

Taking all these things into account, how did our expert assess the changes, if any, in the performance of The Meat-eaters? Well, in the mental tasks and the balance test, there were no real differences between the two groups. But she suggested that they showed a genuine improvement on the physical tests.

In particular, the first three leg extensions in the leg-strength test showed an 11 percent improvement. Strangely, over the full thirty contractions, The Vegetarians actually improved more than The Meat-eaters. In the running tests, it seemed there was no significant result. However, after removing two strange results – one from The Meat-eaters and one from The Vegetarians – there appeared to be a 9 percent improvement.

Our expert suggested that the apparent improvements could be explained by the increased iron levels in The Meat-eaters' diets.

The blood tests confirmed that this group had increased iron levels in their bodies over the three months. She also commented that it could have been due to carnosine from the meat they ate. There were other factors that could have made a difference, positive or negative. For example, during the three months of the experiment, they may not all have trained as hard as each other. A larger and longer-term study would be needed to confirm these results, and to investigate the possible reasons behind them.

So, our experiment points at the tantalizing possibility that eating meat can improve strength and stamina. Of course, there are many accomplished sportsmen and sportswomen – including championship bodybuilders – who are vegetarians. It is fair to say that some of these – the bodybuilders in particular – take creatine or carnosine tablets.

But there are many great athletes who neither eat meat nor take supplements. Carl Lewis has been perhaps the greatest athlete of modern times. In addition to nine Olympic gold medals and one silver, he won eight gold medals in the World Championships in Athletics. Halfway through his career he became a strict vegan, and he continued winning medals. To this day, he eats no animal products at all.

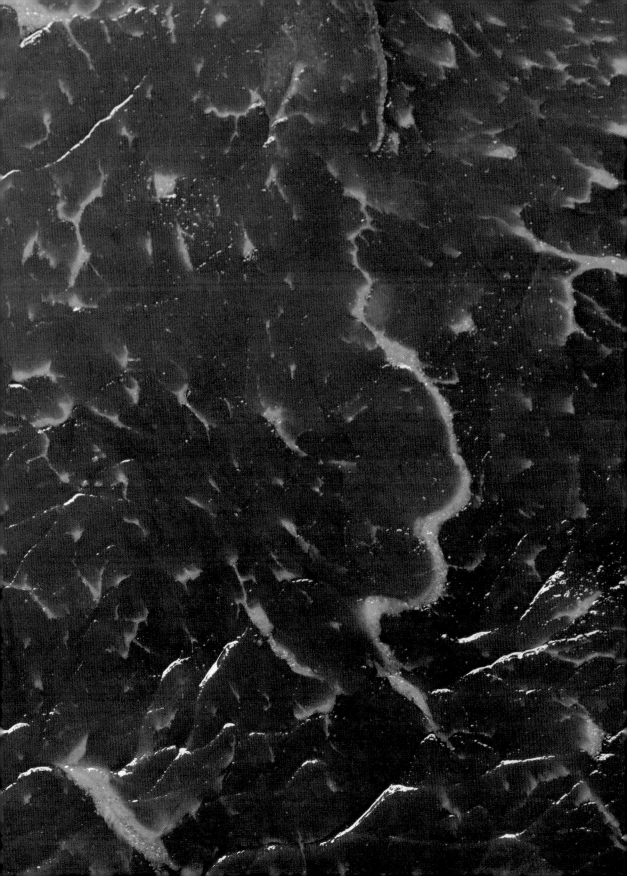

Energy supply:
to graze or to binge?

Polar explorer? Marathon runner? Or simply someone trying your best to get through a busy and physically demanding day? What is the best way to keep performing at your best?

Is it better to have three square meals or to graze little and often? If you are doing physically demanding work, your muscles use up glucose at a much greater rate than usual – and likewise for your brain cells if you are doing mentally demanding work.

Frequent snacks can provide small bursts of glucose into the blood many times a day; the normal three meals a day provide it in just three goes. In that case, the body stores it away, and can easily retrieve it when needed.

So, which is the best strategy? We went to the forests of Montana to meet a man who has dedicated much of his career to finding out.

Within half an hour of eating a sugary snack, all the sugar has broken down into glucose, and that glucose is available to your brain and your muscles – a ready supply of energy.

Sweet things contain "simple sugars," which break down into glucose easily. So, eating something sweet normally means that glucose enters the bloodstream more quickly than it is being used up. When this happens, the body quickly controls the concentration of glucose by raising levels of the hormone insulin. As levels of insulin rise, glucose is quickly stored away as a substance like starch, called glycogen. Most of the glycogen is stored in the liver and the muscles, for use later on.

Any carbohydrates that are not sugars – such as starch – take longer to break down in the gut, but they end up as glucose, too. They will still be trickling glucose into your blood between an hour and four hours later. If you are doing hard work, you will be burning up the calories faster than the food can supply them.

When you are exhausted, or if you haven't eaten for a few hours, your body may have to tap into its stores of glucose – that starchy glycogen in your liver and your muscles.

Glycogen is like your body's reserve

army. When called up, it is quickly broken down into glucose and made available for action. But when glycogen supplies are low, your body begins to break down fats and proteins, and they, too, will produce glucose.

The whole system works well, but it depends upon a precise interplay between glucose, glycogen and insulin. The concentration of insulin determines how much glycogen comes out of store; and the insulin level itself depends upon the concentration of glucose in your blood.

If you know that your brain and your muscles have to keep up a sustained performance for a whole day, it seems sensible to keep topping up glucose levels and not call upon the body's energy storage system. Alternatively, perhaps you should start the day with a carbohydrate-packed breakfast that will release its energy more slowly. Which strategy is best? Does it make any difference?

science jargon buster

Energy from glucose

✲ Glucose fuels every cell in your body – not just brain and muscle cells. In a reaction called cell respiration it combines with oxygen to produce water and carbon dioxide – and a compound called ATP.

✲ It is ATP that your brain and muscle cells actually use as their energy source. Your body can produce ATP directly from proteins and fats, too.

The science test

In the northern USA, lightning causes wildfires, which devour thousands of square miles of pristine forest every year. A large team of dedicated fire fighters keep the blazes at bay as best they can. In the months of July, August and September, they really have their work cut out to keep it all under control. It's not only trees that blaze in the forests of Montana: each working firefighter typically burns between 3,000 and 6,000 kilocalories every day. Supplying energy effectively to these guys throughout the day is crucial.

We ventured to Montana during the wildfire season, to meet Professor Brent Ruby, a physiologist at the University of Montana, Missoula. Professor Ruby is on a quest to find the best diet for people doing extremely strenuous work. As well as being a scientist, he is a triathlete and long-distance runner – so he knows about endurance from his own experience. We caught up with him as he was carrying out a study of firefighters' energy requirements.

Ruby's research has already shown that wildfire fighters' performance tails off mid-afternoon – and that could cost lives, because this is exactly when the fires hit their peak. Ruby has also shown that the immune system suffers during a long, physically draining shift, and that regular carbohydrate top-ups can help to reinforce it.

Traditionally, the firefighters' daytime shift is split into two: they have a big breakfast and a substantial packed lunch. Because of the massive calorie intake required by these hefty firefighters, the packed lunch is three times the size of an ordinary one. The firefighters stop for lunch breaks, during which they try to consume their large lunches.

However, there are problems with this system. For example, the men often don't have time to eat a large meal – and when they do, they normally feel discomfort for the afternoon, after gobbling the meal down at speed. So Ruby and his colleagues developed a system whereby the firefighters could eat a series of small portions on the go. The "First Strike Rations" comprises of eight separate, identical portions, which

REGULAR USERS OF CAFFEINE SUFFER WITHDRAWAL SYMPTOMS WHEN DEPRIVED OF THEIR FAVORITE DRUG.

THE TRUTH ABOUT FOOD

TRUTH ABOUT FOOD NO. 10:
EATING LITTLE AND OFTEN CAN KEEP YOU GOING FOR LONGER.

are to be eaten every ninety minutes, starting ninety minutes after breakfast.

In order to test the effectiveness of the First Strike Rations, Ruby carried out a study that would compare his system with the more traditional feeding approach. During the experiment, firefighters carried their traditional packed lunches one day, and tried the new rations packs the next, as they worked through their twelve-hour shifts. To make the comparison fair, all the men ate breakfast on both days, and the packs and lunches were matched in terms of calorie, protein, fat and carbohydrate content. During the day, each man carried a device that monitored his level of physical activity, and completed a diary sheet of work. At regular intervals, samples were taken, which revealed the concentration of blood glucose.

The results? There was no great difference in the intensity of work overall – probably as a result of the fact that the workload is determined by the fires rather than the feeding patterns. However, Ruby found that men eating the snack-on-the-go ration packs worked 25 percent harder during the last two hours of the demanding twelve-hour shift. By that time, the men who had sat down to lunch had not eaten anything for five hours, while the "snackers" were still topping themselves up. The increased stamina is probably explained by the ready availability of glucose from the small, regular meals, coupled with the fact that the stomach had not had to deal with a large bulk of food in one go.

So, for stamina in a high-energy job, or if you are running a marathon or cycling long distance, drip-feeding energy into your body by grazing regularly on high-carbohydrate foods really seems to work. You don't have to feel bad about that mid-afternoon snack after all – as long as you're doing hard mental or physical work, and as long as you don't simply add snacks to your three meals a day. Keeping overall calorie intake the same, but spreading it out across several small, regular meals, really can increase your stamina.

TOP TIPS – Grazing or bingeing?

1. A high–carbohydrate diet can help you work harder or for longer.
- Eat a carbohydrate-rich meal 2–3 hours before physical activity.
- Top up with a carbohydrate-rich snack thirty minutes before physical activity.
- Refuel with a carbohydrate-rich snack as soon as possible after exercise, ideally, within thirty minutes of finishing.
- Never go hungry or put off eating just because you are too tired.
- Eating late at night is OK – so never go to bed hungry.
- Plan snacks through the day if your job is very physically active.
- Plan ahead. Make sure you always have suitable snacks in store.
- Don't rely on snacks to the exclusion of meals.

2. High glycemic index (GI) carbohydrate-rich foods are a better choice for snacks during and immediately after physical activity. They are absorbed more quickly, and replace used up energy stores sooner than low-GI foods. High glycemic index foods include: instant and mashed potatoes, baked potatoes, watermelon, bread, jelly babies and jelly beans, and sports drinks.

Caffeine:
boost or burden?

Looking for a stimulant that can help you perform better at work and on the sports field? Wake up and smell the coffee.

Whether it's a short, black, bitter espresso or a long, milky, smooth latte, coffee is drunk regularly by millions of people all over the world. Coffee-drinking probably originated in Ethiopia, but it really took off in the Arab world about 1,500 years ago. It reached Europe via Turkey – the first coffeehouse in England was in Oxford and was opened by a Turkish man in 1650.

The active substance in coffee is, of course, the stimulant caffeine. Does caffeine really keep you awake and focused? If you have it every day, does it lose its potency? And what happens if you miss your regular fix?

Caffeine is also said to affect physical performance. It has even been on and off the banned substance list of athletics' World Anti-Doping Agency. We followed twin sisters Lanny and Tracey Barnes – world-class biathletes – as they skied their way across country. Would caffeine help or hinder them?

I like coffee, I like tea

How many of us can't function properly in the morning until we've had our first cup of coffee? Those of you who prefer tea, don't pretend you don't get a caffeine boost as well. Altogether, about sixty plants contain caffeine in their leaves, seeds or roots, where it acts as a natural pesticide.

Coffee and tea are not our only dietary sources of caffeine. Many soft drinks also contain significant amounts. A large glass of cola contains about the same amount as a cup of tea or about half as much as a cup of coffee. Chocolate and other cocoa products also have some. Then there are caffeine pills, mostly used by students trying to stay awake through long hours of study. Some brands contain about two coffees' worth of caffeine per tablet.

Caffeine is absorbed quickly into the bloodstream, directly through the stomach wall and from the small intestine. Most of it will have been absorbed about forty-five minutes after you take that last sip.

If you are a caffeine freak, there is probably always some caffeine in your body. When you drink or eat something containing caffeine, about half of it will have disappeared five or six hours later. By then, you will probably have had some more. Caffeine is "addictive" in the sense that people can easily become dependent on it. It has real withdrawal symptoms that both moderate and heavy users suffer every morning until they get their first fix.

Caffeine hit

As soon as caffeine reaches your bloodstream, it starts doing its thing. In the brain, it blocks the action of a "calming" chemical called adenosine. Your body produces adenosine naturally. It accumulates during the day, and the more concentrated it gets the more you feel like taking a rest.

By bedtime, adenosine is telling your body to sleep. It causes brain cells to slow down – to "go offline" for a while so that repairs can be made. Adenosine also widens blood vessels to the brain, probably to increase blood flow during sleep.

When a caffeine molecule comes into contact with a brain cell, it sits in the spot on the cell membrane reserved for adenosine. That means adenosine can't do its job. So if you would otherwise be drowsy, caffeine will keep you awake. It narrows the blood vessels to the brain, so the heart has to pump harder and faster to keep up with demand.

By blocking the action of adenosine, caffeine also encourages the production of adrenaline – the "fight or flight" hormone produced when you are frightened or excited. This increases your heart rate even more, dilates your pupils, and increases the level of blood sugar.

How much coffee would it take to kill you?

A cup of coffee typically contains about 100 milligrams of caffeine. In the UK and the USA, people typically take in between 200 and 400 milligrams per day. Caffeine is a poison: the lethal dose varies from person to person, but it is normally about 15 grams. To have this much caffeine in your system you would have to drink at least 150 strong cups of coffee over a couple of hours.

Because caffeine takes a while to break down in your body, it can accumulate – but you'd need to drink several cups of coffee every hour for 100 hours or more to reach the lethal dose. So it is almost impossible to die from consuming too much caffeine in drinks, though there have been a few examples of people dying by overdosing on caffeine pills.

If you have about a gram of caffeine – from about ten cups of coffee – coursing through your veins, you will probably feel horribly anxious, jittery and unsettled, your heart racing. But in sensible amounts, caffeine simply makes you feel more alert and focused. People who work erratic hours practically rely on it to carry out their jobs.

You're ready for anything.

As a result of blocking adenosine, caffeine really does make you more alert. But it's not all good news. It seems that, as is true for many drugs, if your body becomes used to it you need to consume caffeine just to function normally. Long-term use seems to make your body produce more adenosine – and that can take a long time to correct.

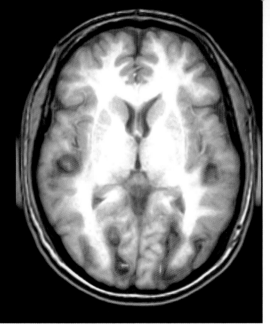 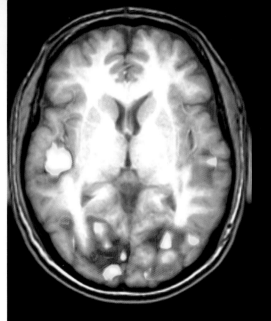

Withdrawing from caffeine can make your brain perform below par – you need to drink caffeine again just to get back to normal. The image on the left shows a brain that has received no caffeine for several days, listening to music and looking at pictures. The regions colored yellow-white are areas of particular activity. The image on the right shows a brain carrying out the same tasks, but which has had its normal caffeine fix. It is much more active. This seems to suggest that caffeine really does improve the brain's performance. But it's not that simple. A "normal" brain – the brain of someone who doesn't use caffeine – would be similar to the picture on the right. In other words, if you have caffeine every day, you have to keep having it just to perform normally. Images kindly supplied by Professor Paul Laurienti from Wake Forest University School of Medicine, North Carolina in association with the Dana Foundation, New York and the National Institutes of Health, Maryland.

Your body still carries on producing adenosine even though caffeine has blocked its action. So when the concentration of caffeine eventually subsides, you will be overloaded with adenosine. Caffeine withdrawal makes you feel really sleepy, and because the blood vessels to your brain widen again, it can give you a nasty headache. Your blood pressure drops, and that can make you feel dizzy and nauseous. Time for another coffee.

There have been many scientific studies into the effects of caffeine. But it can be difficult to achieve meaningful results. At the outset, the volunteers have to have virtually no caffeine in their blood, so that the researchers can compare performance before and after caffeine. Without caffeine in their blood, the volunteers will be suffering withdrawal and will perform worse than if they had never consumed caffeine. Once they have some caffeine, their performance is bound to improve.

As a result, some studies have insisted that their volunteers abstain for at least three days before the experiment. But for heavy, long-term users, this may not be enough to eradicate the effects of withdrawal because they may be over-sensitized to adenosine. So nobody really knows how much habitual caffeine users benefit from their drug of choice.

Caffeine for the Cup

World-class athletes are wary of consuming too much caffeine – but not because it degrades their performance. In fact, it can increase athletic performance considerably.

The reason why top athletes are careful is because they don't want to become dependent on high levels of caffeine when there is a possibility that it will become a banned substance again. The World Anti-Doping Agency's ban on caffeine was lifted in 2004, but it remains on their "monitoring" list. And the International Olympic Committee has set limits on caffeine, so that about five or six cups of strong coffee before an Olympic event could lead to disqualification.

The effect of caffeine on exercise has been studied since the 1970s. Caffeine appears to improve endurance, and seems to work best in activities lasting between half an hour and two hours. It is best taken about an hour before the exercise begins.

No one really knows why caffeine has these effects, but there are several possibilities. Part of the reason is probably because caffeine increases heart rate and boosts adrenaline. It is also known that some of the compounds produced by the breakdown of caffeine can increase heart and lung efficiency. And those same compounds can break down fats, releasing a chemical called glycerol into the bloodstream that can be converted to fuel for your muscles.

Recently, another possibility has come to light. In 2005, Asker Jeukendrup, Professor of Exercise Metabolism at Birmingham University, compared the performance of cyclists who had drunk water with glucose; or water with glucose and caffeine mixed; or just water. The combination of caffeine and glucose worked best.

The science test

Caffeine has been on and off the banned substances list in world-class athletics. So, can it do anything for your physical performance? Is it worth having a strong coffee before you go to the gym or play that game of football or tennis?

It is known that caffeine speeds the absorption of glucose from the intestines. Professor Jeukendrup has suggested that this can make more glucose available to your muscles. We worked with him while planning our own experiment, which took us to the Rocky Mountains in North America. We were lucky to sign up 23-year-olds Lanny and Tracey Barnes – both extremely fit and capable athletes, neither of whom is a regular coffee drinker.

The twins are identical in appearance, and also in performance. In the cross-country skiing event, they normally finish within a second of each other – over a grueling 9-kilometer (5-mile) course.

We gave one of the twins normal coffee and the other decaffeinated coffee before they skied cross-country in a two-hour time trial. Would caffeine make any difference?

We made sure that there was no caffeine in the two women's bodies before the trial began, by prohibiting caffeine-containing products for a week. This would be long enough for any caffeine withdrawal to have come and gone – although neither twin is a coffee drinker anyway. For the twelve hours before the test, we made sure that the twins ate the same food – they kept to their normal pre-competition diet.

The twins' time trials began fifteen minutes apart – this was done to avoid sibling rivalry, which could have been a factor if they were racing against each other. Each woman drank a cup of coffee one hour before her trial, one cup just before setting off, and another halfway through the trial. Lanny's coffees were all decaffeinated – she consumed a total of about 30 milligrams of caffeine. Tracey drank ordinary, strong, "caffeinated" coffees – consuming a total of about 450 milligrams of the drug.

We expected that Tracey would outperform her sister, managing to ski an extra few kilometers in the two-hour trial. But the results were completely opposite to our expectations. In fact, Lanny skied 27.8 kilometers (16.6 miles), while Tracey only managed 24.5 kilometers (14.7 miles) – more than 10 percent less. We made sure that we had given the right coffee to the right twin – so what could explain this result, which is at odds with several other studies?

The twins had their own theory to explain the mysterious result. Although there were only fifteen minutes between the twins' departure times, it was early morning, and the snow was melting. They both agreed that Lanny probably had preferable skiing conditions.

Professor Jeukendrup suggested that a repeated test, in which Tracey left first, would be desirable. He also commented that scientific investigations into the effects of caffeine normally use caffeine supplements, rather than caffeine found in coffee. Of course, there are many other factors that could have played a part in the result when there were only two people involved.

Unlike our experiment, most studies show that caffeine can enhance performance – both mental and physical. It can stave off those tired feelings and keep you alert for longer. And it seems to help supply energy to your muscles, and kick your heart and lungs into gear.

For most of us, a reasonable amount of caffeine each day probably helps to get us through the day. But you can easily become habituated to this stimulant. This could mean that you only perform as well as you would if you never had any.

Strong or weak

Caffeine levels in popular drinks vary greatly. A UK Food Standards Agency survey published in 2001 measured the caffeine content of drinks prepared in homes and offices, and found, for example, that a cup of ordinary instant coffee could contain as little as 21 or as much as 120 milligrams of caffeine. The average figures below were published in that report.

Source	Caffeine content
Average cup of brewed coffee	100mg
Average mug of instant coffee	100mg
Regular energy drink	Up to 80mg
Average cup of instant coffee	75mg
Average cup of tea	50mg
Plain chocolate bar	Up to 50mg – milk chocolate has around half the caffeine content of plain chocolate
Regular cola drink	Up to 40mg

Omega-3: fish for brains

Slabs of wild salmon, fresh from the Pacific, slightly blackened in the pan but still rose pink. Sardines straight off the boat cooking on an open grill on a Portuguese beach, the sun setting, then eaten with crusty bread and a splash of lemon. The unmistakable smell of mackerel, kippers and wood smoke drifting from a fisherman's hut on the Kent coast.

Ah, oily fish! These fishy fantasies are nothing like the oily fish many people remember from their youth. A teaspoon of cod-liver oil to ward off cold bugs; sandwiches made with squashed canned sardines in a strange red sauce for school lunch.

Cod-liver oil and canned sardines probably put some people off oily fish for life. If you are one of those people, you might want to reconsider. Oily fish is one of the really-good-for-you foods. Mackerel and other oily fish are the best source of a very important component of your diet: omega-3.

In terms of long-term brainpower, omega-3 does seem to have a very positive effect, and eating oily fish is the best way to get it. Not only does it enhance brain performance,

it also seems to help us cope better with stress.

We took to the streets of London to investigate. Who could be more stressed than a London cabbie – the noise, the traffic jams, bad drivers and angry passengers demanding to be on time. Would omega-3 help cabbies feel less stressed in this chaos? Then we tried to find out if oily fish could improve the cabbies' memories.

Science fact

A healthy human brain is nearly 10 percent omega-3.

Something fishy

In the UK, we eat more than twice as much white fish as oily fish. Cod, hake and haddock sit proudly on millions of dinner plates across the country, while canned herring, mackerel and sardines languish in the kitchen cupboard.

Other sources of omega-3

If you don't eat fish, you can still get the omega-3 you need. Good vegetable sources are walnuts, rapeseed oil and flaxseeds. A glass of organic milk – from cows fed on clover – provides 10 percent of the recommended daily intake (RDI) of ALA, while a matchbox-sized piece of organic cheese will give you up to 88 percent.

Oiling your brain

Fatty acids are an important constituent of cell membranes. The membrane of a cell keeps everything inside – like the stretched rubber skin of a water-filled balloon. And having the right kinds of fatty acids in the cell membrane is particularly important in brain cells.

Omega-3 is a polyunsaturated fatty acid – you may have seen this name on food labels. There is another type of polyunsaturated fatty acid present in your diet, and in your body: omega-6. This is present in large quantities in many of the foods we eat. For example, it is present in wheat, vegetable oil, eggs, poultry and grain-fed meat.

The diet of early humans was quite different. They ate more fish, and meat from animals that had eaten grass, so they took in about the same amounts of omega-6 and omega-3. Nowadays, in the West at least, most people consume ten or twenty times as much omega-6 as omega-3. This is largely a result of intensive agriculture and processed foods. Levels of omega-3 in our diet have never been so low.

Well, the time has come for oily fish everywhere to stand up and be counted. Packed into their cells is, well, oil. And that oil contains omega-3.

Oily fish are not the only source of omega-3. White fish also have it, but it ends up concentrated in their livers – cod-liver oil contains a whopping 20 percent omega-3. But you shouldn't rely solely on cod-liver oil for your intake, because you might inadvertently take in too much vitamin A and vitamin D, which cod-liver oil also contains in abundance. You can get omega-3 from a range of foods other than fish – see the box below.

Fatty acids

Omega-3 is an example of a fatty acid – a key component of fats and oils. It is a polyunsaturated fatty acid – you may have seen this on food labels.

Actually, the name omega-3 doesn't refer to just one fatty acid: there are dozens of them. Three of them are particularly important to us – they are normally referred to by the abbreviations ALA, EPA and DHA.

Of these three omega-3 fatty acids, we absolutely must have ALA in our diet: it is known as an "essential fatty acid" because the human body can't manufacture it. We can make the other two – from ALA – but not very efficiently. It is best to make sure you have all three in your diet.

ALA is present in a range of foods, but the other two are only really found in fish oils, and in human breast milk.

This is a big deal because research suggests that the disturbed ratio of omega-6 to omega-3 may be partly to blame for the apparent rise in brain-related problems – including aggression, depression, and even autism and Alzheimer's disease. In many studies, increasing people's intake of omega-3 has helped people suffering from these conditions. And plenty of studies indicate that omega-3 can improve children's memory and concentration, even over a matter of weeks.

An intriguing British study, whose results were published in 2002, studied the effects of dietary supplements on violent young offenders in a high-security prison. Omega-3 was one of the most prominent nutrients used in the study. More than 200 people were involved, only half of whom received the supplements. After twenty weeks, the group that had received the supplements committed 24 percent fewer offenses in the prison than the control group, which received placebos.

Everyone agrees that getting enough omega-3 is very important. But most studies into the positive effects of omega-3 on the brain have focused either on people with unhealthy brains, like those with Alzheimer's disease, or on the developing brains of babies and children. It is clearly very important to eat omega-3 when you are healing your brain or building it from scratch. But what about everyone else? Can it improve your performance?

The science tests

We decided to find out if an increased intake of omega-3 would make a difference to healthy, adult brains. There is some evidence that omega-3 can improve memory and reduce stress, but it is still largely unproven. So in two separate experiments, we focused on people for whom increased memory and reduced stress would be very welcome: London cabbies.

We recruited ten cabbies who rarely ate oily fish. For twelve weeks, we feed them four portions of oily fish each week. Before and after the three-month period, we carried out memory tests and evaluated their stress levels. Helping us in our experiments was Dr. Alex Richardson, senior research fellow at the Department of Physiology, Anatomy and Genetics at the University of Oxford. Dr. Richardson has carried out several important studies into the links between nutrition on behavior and learning, including the effects of omega-3.

Total recall

The drivers of London's iconic black cabs are well known for being chatty; many of them are unstoppable storytellers. But they also need excellent brains because learning all of London's thousands of streets and alleyways can take up to three years of hard training. To pass the test at the end of it – called "the Knowledge" – they need to have built up a detailed street map of Greater London in their head.

We assessed our volunteers' memory abilities using a standard and very straightforward test: we gave them series of numbers to remember. We also gave them a fictional route to remember. On the number recall test, five of our cabbies actually did very slightly worse at the end of the twelve weeks. But on average, scores increased very slightly. However, in the other test, all but one of our volunteers showed significant improvement: the average improvement of memory was a whopping 25 percent. This was a small study, and you can't draw too many conclusions – but there really seemed to be an increase in the cabbies' performance as the result of eating oily fish.

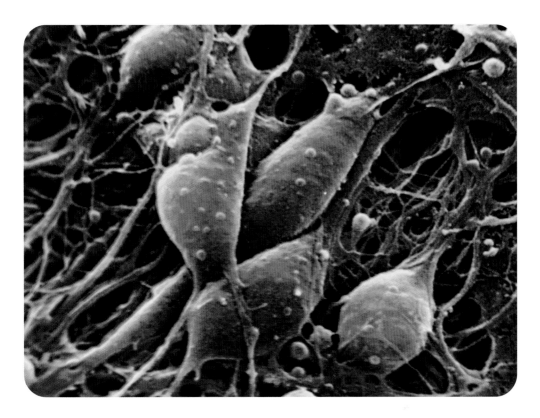

Our thoughts and memories depend upon electrical impulses passing between nerve cells, or neurons. The cell body, colored yellow in this scanning electron microscope image, contains the cell nucleus and other important features. Extensions of the cell reach out to other neurons. Each neuron is surrounded by a membrane rich in omega-3 fatty acids. The human brain contains around 100 billion neurons, each connected to an average of 7,000 others.

Stress-free streets?

In the second test, we determined the same group's stress levels over a twenty-four-hour period: during a normal working shift and while they slept. To do this, we tracked variations in their heart rate. This is relatively easy to do, and is recognized as a very accurate way to measure stress and overall health. We called in heart specialist Dr. Alan Watkins to carry out the tests for us. Each of our volunteers wore a "stressometer" around his or her arm, which picked up the heart's electrical activity. A box strapped around the waist recorded the electrodes' signals for the full twenty-four hours.

We also measured levels of the "stress hormone" cortisol and the "anti-stress hormone" DHEA (dehydroepiandrosterone) in the cabbies' saliva, which we sampled four times during the day.

As you might expect, our cab drivers were on very short fuses. Having to deal with the madness of London's roads day after day can do that to you. Throughout each day of testing, we put our cabbies under additional pressure: we sent an actor into the cabs to wind up the drivers. We asked the actor to behave obnoxiously and to pretend he was on the verge of throwing up.

Other studies have shown that omega-3 can have a positive effect on mood, but some scientists in the field remain unconvinced. So what results did we get in our little study?

Dr. Watkins performed a careful analysis of the drivers' heart-rate variability, and gave each a stress rating, based on a recognized system. Two of the volunteers showed no real change, and one did not take the test the second time, but all the rest showed significant improvements in their ratings after the twelve weeks. The tests we carried out on the saliva went along with these results – it really seems the oily fish made a difference.

The results of our tests before and after twelve weeks of intensive fish eating seem to suggest that oily fish really can make a difference to mental performance and to our ability to cope with stress. And we managed to convert several of our cabbies to the joys of oily fish – they told us that mackerel, salmon and sardines would now become regular visitors on their dinner plates.

TOP TIPS – Omega-3

Adults should aim to consume 0.45g of omega-3 a day, or just over 3g a week. Average consumption is estimated at only half this amount. The recommended intake can be achieved simply by including oily fish in the weekly diet.

1. Oily fish:
- salmon, sardines and mackerel (fresh or canned)
- trout
- herring
- tuna steak (but not canned)

The basic recommendation is to eat at least 280g of fish a week (equivalent to two portions) of which one portion must be an oily fish.

- Girls under sixteen years of age, pregnant women or those who may become pregnant and breastfeeding women should have no more than two portions of oily fish a week.

- Other women, men and boys can eat up to four portions a week.

2. Other sources of omega-3 include walnuts, rapeseeds, soybean, flaxseeds and dark green vegetables – all items that may not be eaten on a regular basis or in sufficient amounts to meet requirements.

- Using rapeseed, soybean or walnut oils for cooking or salad dressings can help to boost intake.
- Lamb, venison and dark chicken meat (i.e. not the breast) contain small amounts of omega-3 too.
- Eggs laid by hens consuming diets rich in omega-3 (e.g. Columbus eggs) and bread fortified with omega-3 (a food which could be eaten on a daily basis) can certainly help push up overall weekly intakes.

Sugar kick:
mind over matter

We've all felt that afternoon tiredness thing – where everything becomes a bit too much trouble and you just want to curl up and sleep. You may have noticed that a cake or chocolate bar can quickly pick you up.

That snack picks you up almost as soon as you put it in your mouth – long before the sugar could possibly have reached your body tissues. It's as if your brain and your muscles are on a promise. Research backs up the idea that you don't even have to swallow the sugar to get a boost. The mere presence of sugar can do the trick.

Over the past twenty years, many scientists studying fatigue have come around to thinking that it happens in – or is even caused by – the brain.

According to traditional scientific wisdom, physical fatigue is caused when your muscles run out of energy, or when they demand oxygen at a greater rate that your body can supply it. Without oxygen, muscles can still do their job, but they produce an acid that accumulates over time. That acid makes your muscles ache.

If this were a total explanation of fatigue, then marathon runners would gradually grind to a halt and would certainly find it very difficult to speed up over the last kilometer – as they almost always do. Somehow, the brain can override what the muscles are telling it.

You know the fuel warning light in a car that comes on when you've still got a good thirty kilometers' worth left? It's not telling you that you've run out of fuel. It's telling you to get some more fuel soon or else there really will be trouble. Your brain does the same, except that, unlike the warning light, it takes control. It makes you shut down.

Our prehistoric ancestors would always have needed a bit of energy in reserve, to run away from danger. And even without danger, there is no reason why the brain would let the body dangerously over-exert itself. It would step in before any permanent damage was done.

This modern theory of exhaustion, which is steadily gaining in popularity, has been called the "central governor" theory. It claims that the brain takes in all the information it can about the rate of exercise, the body's temperature, the efficiency of muscle function and so on – and if it's not satisfied it makes you feel tired.

Athletes report that the first kilometer of a ten-kilometer race is easier than the first kilometer of a five-kilometer race. This can only be explained if the brain is actually partly in control of making you feel fatigued. Amphetamines have been shown to increase physical output during exercise, and yet these are drugs that work on the brain, not the muscles. Even hypnosis can increase your physical endurance. Again, the brain seems to play a central role.

Spit or swallow

These new ideas are backed up by several studies. For example, in tests, athletes improve their performance after sugary drinks, but not after the same amount of sugar is injected directly into their blood. In other words, before any sugar reaches the bloodstream, the mouth sends a message to the brain: "body now refueled."

In another study, cyclists were given either a sugar-rich or sugar-free drink. The drinks didn't taste sugary, so the cyclists were unaware which they had been given. During a time trial, they were told not to swallow the drink but to hold it in their mouth for five seconds, then spit it out.

Very little sugar would have made it into their body, so in theory neither drink should have made any difference to their performance. Yet those who had the sugar-rich drink improved their performance significantly.

These experiments were carried out by Professor David Jones of Birmingham University, who suggests that sensors in the mouth detect the presence of carbohydrates in your mouth, and the brain adjusts the feelings of fatigue accordingly.

The science test

Research suggests that the brain – and not the muscles – controls your feelings of exhaustion. If so, a small snack could really pick you up.

To investigate, we traveled to the West Indian island of Grenada, where we worked with a group of hard-working cane-cutters as they hacked their way through fields of sugar cane. Every fifteen minutes, the workers stopped to take a drink. We split the cutters into three groups: the first group drank just water, the second a carbohydrate-rich drink, and the third had the same carbohydrate drink, but they merely swilled it around their mouth and spat it out – this group also drank water, so that they would not dehydrate.

Each group harvested along five lanes, with two cutters in each lane. Amazingly, both the carbohydrate groups made it to the ends of their lanes at almost exactly the same time – even though in one group, the carbohydrates never made it further than the mouth. The other group, who had only water, was far behind.

If you want to perform at your best, beyond the point at which you would normally become exhausted, an intake of carbohydrates before or during exercise can help you. Our experiment supports Professor Jones' earlier finding: that carbohydrates can help improve your performance – even if you don't digest them. Of course, if your carbohydrate pick-me-up is a doughnut or a small chocolate bar, you'll probably want to swallow, not spit.

Alcohol:
for better and for worse

Somewhere in the world right now, someone is saying "Never again." Since the dawn of civilization, people have enjoyed alcoholic drinks, drunk too much and regretted it the next day.

Have you ever wondered what happens inside your body after a liquid lunch, or after downing a couple of glasses of spirits? Why does alcohol affect your performance – making you dizzy, and unable to do much at all the morning after a heavy session?

The effects of alcohol are well known to most of us, and science can help to explain some of the things we experience.

Drinking it in

Alcohol starts to affect your brain as soon as it reaches your bloodstream. Normally only about 10 percent of alcohol is absorbed into your blood across the wall of the stomach. The other 90 percent passes into the blood, more rapidly, from the small intestine. The contents of your stomach will make a difference.

If you were sensible and consumed a hearty supper before that first drink, then the valve at the bottom of the stomach, called the pyloric sphincter, will stay shut. This holds the food back, giving your stomach a chance to mash it up and mix it with digestive juices. If the alcohol stays in your stomach longer, it will be absorbed more slowly.

But if there is no food, the valve opens to let liquids pass through – there is no need for your stomach to hold back a liquid. This is why you feel the effects of alcohol sooner and more strongly on an empty stomach.

When you drink spirits, you will often experience a delayed but quite sudden "hit." One minute you are thinking that someone must have watered down the whisky, the next everything starts to spin.

This is because strong alcohol irritates the pyloric sphincter at the bottom of the stomach, making it stay firmly shut, and this delays the time it takes for the alcohol to leave the stomach. By the time it finally opens to let the alcohol through, you have probably had two or three drinks. Those drinks will pass rapidly into your bloodstream as soon as they reach your small intestine and go straight to the brain.

Fatty food doesn't "line the stomach"

as many people believe. But it does stimulate the release of a hormone that delays your stomach emptying. So a glass of full-cream milk is not a bad idea before a night out.

Another urban myth is that dried bread will "soak up" the alcohol. A sandwich before alcohol can help to break down the alcohol more quickly if it contains protein and fats, because these nutrients stimulate the production of enzymes that also speed the breakdown of alcohol. With these enzymes in your system, you will get rid of the alcohol more quickly. So, have a cheese sandwich before you go to that party.

If your wine or beer is very fizzy – champagne, for example – the buildup of gas in your stomach will cause the sphincter to open. This is why sparkling wines tend to make you tipsy almost right away.

Women can't hold their liquor

One little-known factor in how quickly alcohol is absorbed, and how quickly it affects you, is gender. There is an enzyme in your stomach that begins to break down alcohol before it even leaves your stomach.

But if you are a woman, you have less of it than men. This is also true of an enzyme in your liver – the main organ of detoxification. Until the liver can break it down, alcohol continues to circulate in your bloodstream, doing its thing. Yes, women tend to get drunker quicker.

All in your head

So what does alcohol actually do inside your body? It's no surprise that the main effects are in your head – and that doesn't mean you just imagine them. Once in your blood, the alcohol is carried around all your body tissues, but it is in your brain that it has the most striking effects.

First, alcohol increases levels of a neurotransmitter called dopamine. A neurotransmitter is a compound that plays a crucial role in how your brain cells communicate with each other. Dopamine is particularly active in the brain's pleasure center, and this is why the first symptom of being inebriated is euphoria. You feel good after the first couple of drinks. The problem is you often want more.

If you increase your blood alcohol concentration – by having another drink – the alcohol begins to make you feel sleepy. Alcohol is a depressant: it interferes directly with the chemical reactions that make your brain cells produce electrical signals. In other words it reduces the electrical activity of your brain, making you drowsy and less able to concentrate.

Drink any more and the alcohol disturbs more and more areas of your brain, including those that control your balance and temperature regulation, and those that control how much you urinate. You may lose the ability to stand and to talk, your vision becomes blurred, and you may feel an irresistible compulsion to crawl to the toilet and vomit.

Alcohol is a toxin and despite its pleasurable effects at the beginning of the evening, your body wants rid of it. About 5 percent of the alcohol you imbibe is expelled by the kidneys – you urinate it out. A similar amount evaporates into the air from your lungs – you breathe it out. As a result, the concentration of alcohol in your breath is an accurate measure of the concentration of alcohol in your blood.

The main features of a hangover are a banging headache and extreme fatigue.

Alcohol robs your brain of water. It is a diuretic, which means that you urinate much more water than you take in. The resulting dehydration makes your brain shrink from the inside of your skull slightly, giving you that throbbing pain. Alcohol also robs your brain of glucose by interrupting processes that release this important fuel into the blood. This makes you lackluster and unable to do very much apart from feel very sorry for yourself.

As your brain cells begin to recover their normal function, you become over-sensitized to light and sound. The glare of the morning sunlight and the crashing of the cutlery in the kitchen can be unbearable.

Dark drinks

Some alcoholic beverages seem to give you worse hangovers than others. Scientific studies highlight darker drinks like brandy and red wine as the biggest culprits. Darker drinks contain more congeners – impurities that are produced during fermentation – and they worsen your hangover.

Feeling better?

So what about hangover cures? People try many different ways to make themselves feel better, or try to speed up their recovery from a hangover. It can become a bit of a mission.

One favorite in Britain is the fried breakfast: fried eggs, bacon, mushrooms and tomatoes, with lots of toast or fried bread. Fried foods like these contain lots of salt and amino acids. Your body needs salt after urinating and sweating so much; and the amino acids help to get the liver back on track after it has worked so hard to expel all that alcohol. A big breakfast will also boost your blood glucose, helping you to shake off that tiredness.

In Germany, most people opt for a fruit smoothie. Made with fresh fruit, this drink provides vitamin C, which helps the liver to process

the last of the alcohol, and the liquid content helps you rehydrate.

Some people rely on "the hair of dog that bit you." In other words, more alcohol. A favorite in the USA is a Bloody Mary (vodka and tomato juice). Drinking yet more alcohol may seem like a crazy idea, but it can actually stop the breakdown of congeners – substances in alcoholic drinks that make a hangover worse (see "Dark drinks"). Sadly, though, it's more like pressing a pause button: as soon as the new alcohol has gone, the hangover continues.

A strong coffee may make you more alert, but if you are running on empty, it won't actually alleviate any of the symptoms of your hangover. Some painkillers will also help – at least they reduce the pain of your headache. But ideally you should try to avoid taking medications when alcohol is still present in your body. If they are depressant medications, like codeine or tranquilizers, then combining them with alcohol can be dangerous.

Drinking pure water when you have a hangover is fine, but your body may react as if its fluids are becoming too diluted: you will probably urinate most of it straight out. Sports drinks contain electrolytes that replace those lost by excessive urinating the night before, and probably a few times during the night. These drinks don't disturb your body's electrolyte balance, so they can rehydrate it quite efficiently.

There are countless other supposed hangover cures. You can even buy ones specially designed to supply everything that your body has lost as a result of drinking too much. But no hangover cure is a magic formula. Your body has most of what it requires: it just needs time to do its thing. You can help it along by drinking water, and by resting.

Spending most of the day horizontal under your duvet will also give you ample time to repeat the hangover mantra: "Never again."

SUMMARY: HOW TO BE THE BEST

 Vegetarians don't miss out on much, as long as they have a varied and balanced diet; but there is some evidence that low intakes of iron and a compound called carnosine may affect athletic performance.

 FOR PHYSICAL OR MENTAL STAYING POWER, IT IS A GOOD IDEA TO DRIP-FEED ENERGY INTO YOUR BODY, BY GRAZING REGULARLY ON HIGH-CARBOHYDRATE FOODS.

Caffeine makes you more alert, and there is evidence that it helps physical performance, too; but if you are a regular user, you may have to keep up your intake just to perform to your normal level.

 OILY FISH IS THE BEST SOURCE OF OMEGA-3 FATTY ACIDS, WHICH CAN REDUCE STRESS AND IMPROVE MEMORY.

 Fatigue may be as much to do with the brain and the mind as the muscles; the mere taste of sugary food can increase a tired athlete's performance.

6. HOW TO STAY YOUNG AND BEAUTIFUL

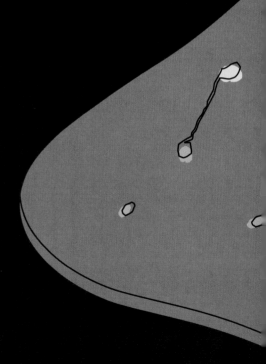

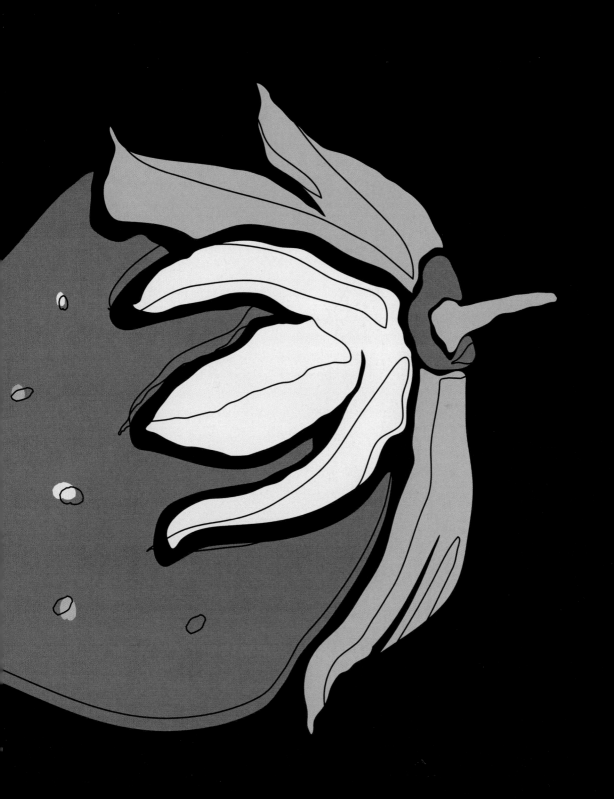

HOW TO STAY YOUNG AND BEAUTIFUL

Day after day, our incredible bodily machinery sparks and pumps away, generating and regenerating cells and tissues, maintaining the most sophisticated organism on the planet. For most of us most of the time, year after year, it all works. We are healthy. And we want to stay that way for as long as possible.

In 1901, a woman's life expectancy in England was forty-nine years. Now, just over a hundred years later, it's around eighty-two years. And it's continuing to increase, still going up by eighteen months every decade.

This is an amazing trend. As I write this book, I am fifty-eight years old. If I had lived a hundred years ago, I could well have been rotting in my grave for years already. Today, I'm planning on working full-time for another ten years, then hiking and skiing through my seventies and into my eighties.

I like it that I'm going to live a lot longer than previous generations. But I don't want to become an on-the-shelf oldie. I want to keep on living, for as long as possible, as an energetic, sharp-minded, healthy person.

My daughter is in her mid-twenties but she is as concerned about managing the aging process as I am. She wants the skin and hair of a twenty-year-old, not a thirty-year-old. She knows her lifestyle choices now will affect her chances of staying young and beautiful in her thirties and forties.

In the past few decades, our understanding of the biological mechanisms behind aging has advanced in leaps and bounds. We can all feel much more empowered to take control of our own aging destiny. Aging, like death and taxes, may be inevitable, but we really can influence how rapidly it advances.

So, what causes aging? According to the most widely accepted scientific theory, chemical agents called "free radicals" are the main culprits. Free radicals are the body's vandals. They wreak havoc inside our cells, causing damage that can't always be mended. To most scientists, the accumulation of free radical damage over time is what aging is all about.

The first good way to deal with the free radical problem is to stop encouraging their production. This means refraining from things like smoking and sun worshipping. In my New Zealand youth in the 1950s, I burnt myself to a crisp like every other bikinied teenager, and I'm paying the price now in wrinkles, brown patches on my skin and worries about melanomas.

The second good way is to mop them up with "antioxidants" as fast as possible when they have been produced. This is where knowing the truth about food comes in. The right foods are amazingly powerful weapons in the fight against free radicals and aging. In this chapter we'll look at some of our greatest antioxidant allies: berries, tomatoes, spinach and red wine (thank God for red wine!). We'll look at how they can help keep us young and beautiful – on the outside and on the inside.

Berries:
food for thought

It is true that when it comes to keeping your brain young, it's a case of "use it or lose it." But even if you carry on exercising your mind into your later years, your brain will age. And as you move toward that part of life where "senior moments" become commonplace, you need to work harder just to keep up.

Free radicals attack the cells in your brain just as they do elsewhere in your body, and the damage tends to accumulate. You can fight back – and a handful of blueberries each day might just provide the ammunition you need.

If good things come in small packages, the blueberry is a perfect example. With such a dark color and bursting with intense zesty flavors, it is no surprise that blueberries are packed with goodness and are a top choice for a healthy diet.

Berry nice

Blueberries have grown wild in Asia and North America for many thousands of years. The wild variety is nutritionally best as the berries are smaller. The antioxidant content is greater in a small berry, because the antioxidants are concentrated in the skin. North America now boasts the largest production of blueberries – more of the world's wild blueberries are grown in Canada than anywhere else. A close relative of the blueberry, called the bilberry, grows in Europe. Cranberries are also part of the same family.

Researchers have found that eating these berries, and blueberries in particular, can reduce the amount of "bad" cholesterol in the blood, and cut the risk of certain cancers. They can even stave off urinary tract infections. But it is their possible role in keeping brains and minds young that is proving most exciting.

The deep blue color of fresh blueberries is due to anthocyanin pigment – a powerful antioxidant that fights those free radicals. Just half a cup of blueberries contain the same quantity of antioxidants as five servings of peas, broccoli, carrots or apples.

Young brains on old shoulders

There is a myth that after you reach the age of thirty you lose 100,000 brain cells every day, and that no new ones can form. Thankfully this really is a myth. Brain cells do die, but new ones are made all the time and, throughout your life, new connections form between them. Researchers have shown that, structurally at least, the brain of a sixty-year-old is not really any different from that of a twenty-year-old. In adulthood, the brain actually shrinks by about 2 percent each decade, but that doesn't mean that it can't do its job just as well. More importantly, studies suggest that new brain cells are being generated into or even beyond a person's eighties.

Nowadays, more people live to a ripe old age than ever before. The over-seventies are rapidly becoming the fastest growing age group. In the next few decades, the children of the post-war baby boom will be retiring and growing old. Mental decline is likely to be one of their greatest fears.

Nobody wants to lose their faculties: to become slow, confused, unable to make new memories – or, worse still perhaps, unable to retrieve old ones. We are all horribly aware of Alzheimer's disease and other forms of dementia, which affect more than a quarter of all people over age eighty. But even without specific conditions like these, there is a general "cognitive decline" associated with old age – isn't there?

On average, people in their eighties do worse than those in their twenties or thirties in mental tests involving short-term memory, mental arithmetic and multitasking. "On average," yes – but there are many octogenarians who perform just as well as their younger counterparts. It seems that some people can postpone the aging inside their brains. But what is it they are postponing? What physical changes cause mental decline?

Inflammation overload

Like all tissues in the body, the brain has a defense against unwanted intruders: that defense is called inflammation. Useful though it is, we are often annoyed by inflammation when it occurs in a place where we can see and feel it. Inflammation increases blood flow, which puts pressure on nearby nerve endings and makes the inflamed area throb with pain. We can't feel inflammation in the brain because there are no pain sensors there. But it does happen. Allergies, the presence of toxins, stress and even a diet low in essential nutrients can cause the brain to become inflamed.

An important part of the process of inflammation is the immune response – the recruitment of a SWAT team to attack foreign bacteria or other undesirables. In the brain, this SWAT team consists of cells called microglia (in the rest of the body, it is white blood cells). Part of their offensive involves producing vicious free radicals, which bump off undesirable invaders. But it seems that the free radicals they produce also damage the very cells they are supposed to protect – and this may be a major feature of aging brains.

As well as fighting off invaders, microglia have a more mundane role: they act as the brain's caretakers, clearing up debris left behind when cells are damaged or die. Once the microglia have been scrambled into action, they tend to cluster around a protein substance called amyloid, which builds up between brain cells. Again, they produce free radicals in a vain attempt to clear it away. The free radicals have

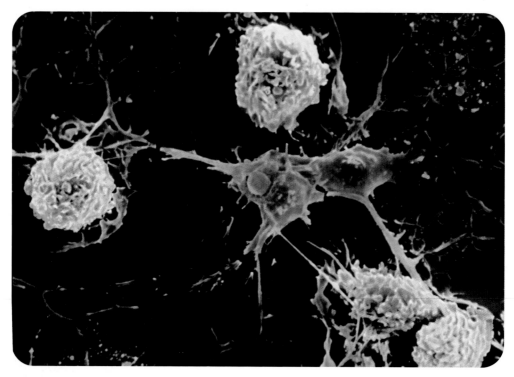

This picture, taken using a scanning electron microscope, shows the brain's immune system workers, microglial cells, in yellow, attacking a brain cell. This is what happens in the brains of sufferers of multiple sclerosis; the damage results in loss of nerve function. Microglia seem to play an important role in brain aging, too. When they attack free radicals in the brain, as part of the immune response, they can attack healthy brain cells.

no effect on the amyloid, but the microglia continue to produce more and more of them. And so it goes – on and on, the resulting cycle producing more and more free radicals. The brains of people with any type of dementia contain more microglia than the brains of those without, and older people's brains contain more microglia than younger people's.

Radical solution

So how can you keep your brain young? The inflammation and free radical damage that takes its toll on our brains may seem inevitable and rather scary. But evidence gathered over several decades shows that by eating fruit and vegetables we can slow down the slide into damage and aging. A healthy diet may even reduce the risk of developing dementia-type diseases such as Alzheimer's disease.

In particular, berries contain large amounts of compounds called polyphenols (also called polyphenolics), which fight aging in the brain in two ways. First, polyphenols are powerful antioxidants, which mop up the harmful free radicals. Second, they have natural anti-inflammatory properties, and by inflammation they decrease the numbers of microglia produced, which may reduce the aging effect.

Researchers have long realized that people taking anti-inflammatory drugs, such as aspirin, over long periods of time have reduced risk of dementia. It seems that the same may apply to natural anti-inflammatory substances.

Polyphenols are hot news in aging research. There are around 5,000 varieties of these chemical compounds, found in most fruits and vegetables. But berries – and blueberries in particular – have gained most attention.

Colorful chemicals

Polyphenols are a class of chemical compound produced in plants. Red wine, tea and dark chocolate are good sources of polyphenols. There is growing evidence from research that these compounds help to protect against heart disease and cancers.

In 1999, researchers at the Human Nutrition Research Center on Aging in Boston, Massachusetts, announced that they had significantly improved rats' brainpower by feeding them blueberries. Since then, thousands of laboratory rats have been given blueberries or blueberry extracts in an attempt to find out more. These experiments seem to confirm that blueberries are indeed a super-brain-food. They improve elderly rats' balance and coordination, they dramatically reduce damage in the brains of rats that have had strokes, and speed the animals' recovery afterward. There is even evidence that polyphenols from blueberries encourage the animals' brains to generate new brain cells.

Since 2000, researchers have achieved some similar results in humans. One two-year trial involved senior citizens carrying out memory and reaction tests over the Internet. Volunteers were randomly assigned to groups receiving daily doses of either blueberries or other foods. The blueberry group showed a 4.2 percent improvement in their cognitive ability – more than twice the improvement in the other groups.

It really seems that berries and other fruits and vegetables might help us think younger for longer. It would be nice to believe that every one of us could have a long and fruitful life – or, at least, a long life full of fruit.

TOP TIPS – Berries

Enjoy a portion of berries every day, as part of your daily five portions of fruits and vegetables: 2–3 heaped tablespoons of berries is roughly equivalent to an 80g portion.

Antioxidant rating per serving	Berries or fruit
Best	Apple (Golden Delicious, Granny Smith, Red Delicious), blackberry, blueberry, cherry, cranberry, plum, raspberry, strawberry
Very good	Apricot, red or green grapes, red grapefruit, orange, peach, pear, tangerine
Good	Banana, kiwi fruit, mango, nectarine
OK	Cantaloupe melon, watermelon

Red wine:
an affair of the heart?

In 2002, Professor Roger Corder of St. Bartholomew's Hospital in London went to Sardinia to meet a group of centenarians and find out the secret of their long and healthy lives. In particular, he wanted to find out what type of red wine they drank.

Other scientists also believe that chemicals found in red wine can help to reduce the risk of heart disease. They determined to find out which chemicals they are, and exactly how they work.

Ancient tipple

The very first wine was almost certainly made by accident, since the yeast necessary for fermentation grows naturally on grape skins. In the ancient world, fermentation was one of the few ways to preserve food against spoiling – together with salting, drying, smoking and pickling.

People have been making wine for at least 5,000 years, and today it is a multi-billion-dollar industry. Worldwide, about 8 million hectares (20 million acres) of land is devoted to the cultivation of grapes – that's a little more than the total area of Scotland. Around 30 million liters (7 million gallons) of wine were sold globally in 2005.

Despite claims for health benefits from drinking red wine, it should not be forgotten that excessive consumption of alcohol has very many negative effects. In the UK, twice as many people are dependent on alcohol as all other drugs put together (including prescription drugs but not including nicotine). Excessive intake of alcohol increases the risk of liver disease as well as heart disease. It can wreck relationships and make people behave violently. One in six visits to hospital emergency rooms is directly related to alcohol, and one in seven people killed on the roads is involved in a drunk-driving accident. According to official figures, about a quarter of men and one-sixth of women drink more than the recommended safe amounts. If red wine really does have health benefits, then moderation is clearly the key.

Some people are confused about the real difference between white wine and red wine. White wine can be made with green, red or black

grapes, but the skins are not included during fermentation. Red wine, on the other hand, is only made with red or black grapes, but the skins are mixed in with the juice during fermentation. This gives red wine its color, contributes to its flavor, and – perhaps most importantly – makes red wine a far more complex mixture than white wine.

Surprisingly, perhaps, red wine is rich in antioxidants. In particular, it contains chemicals called flavonoids. Certain flavonoids – the proanthocyanidins – are particularly exciting. It is already known that proanthocyanidins help to prevent the breakdown of collagen molecules in skin – a major cause of skin aging.

Grapes with thicker skins – normally hardier varieties grown at higher altitudes – tend to produce red wine containing more flavonoids. Also, the longer the grapes' skins are left in with the grape juice at the beginning of the winemaking process, the more flavonoids will make it into the finished product. And flavonoids – proanthocyanidins in particular – are the compounds that Professor Corder and other researchers believe reduce the risk of heart disease.

Too many broken hearts

Diseases of the heart claim more lives than anything else, and most of the people who die from heart disease are killed by heart attacks. In the UK alone, around 275,000 people suffer a heart attack every year – that's one every two minutes. About 120,000 people die every year as a result. Heart attacks cause one in eight of all deaths worldwide – but more than one in four in developed nations.

Nearly all heart attacks are due to "cardiovascular" disease: problems with the heart (*cardio*) and blood vessels (*vascular*). This begins with a buildup of fatty material just below the lining of the arteries supplying the heart. These deposits look like yellow fatty streaks and consist mostly of dead white blood cells. The cells find their way into the lining of the arteries as a result of inflammation – part of the body's immune response. As time goes by, these deposits increase in size, with fibers and even bone-like tissues growing over them. This is why the process is sometimes called "hardening of the arteries."

These growths in the artery eventually begin to restrict the flow – just as limescale does in water pipes. This reduction in blood flow can deprive the heart of oxygen and often leads to angina – a pain or discomfort in the chest and down the arms. Angina is usually a warning sign that more trouble is on the way.

Ultimately, the strain on the narrowed blood vessels can rupture them. The body's response to this is to clot the blood at the site of the damage, but the clot can completely block the artery, preventing blood from reaching the heart muscle at all. The muscle cells quickly become starved of oxygen and begin to die.

Risk factors

Most of the people who die from heart attacks are over seventy-five, and most of them are also suffering from other diseases. In fact, "dying of old age" most often involves heart disease – and we all have to go sometime. But younger people should not be complacent. Cardiovascular disease is also the major cause of premature death, and many middle-aged people are at risk.

The key factor in the development of cardiovascular disease is the buildup of the material that narrows the arteries. This is almost impossible to detect from outside the body until it has become extremely serious. In most cases, a sudden heart attack is the first symptom. The material builds up gradually over several decades, beginning as early as five years of age. But it does not accumulate at the same rate in everyone. Damage to the lining of the arteries – by free radicals or high blood pressure – seems to speed it up.

Smoking raises blood pressure and produces lots of free radicals – it is a major risk factor for heart disease. Stress raises blood pressure. In addition, cholesterol seems to play an important role; it leaks into the artery lining from the bloodstream. The best way to reduce your risk of heart disease is to make a few key changes in your lifestyle. Take plenty of exercise, avoid food high in saturated fat, and stay away from stress and cigarettes. But there is another thing you could do: live a rural existence in the south of France.

Looking for clues

In 1819, an Irish doctor named Samuel Black noted that the French – despite their love of meat, cream, butter, cheese and wine – tended to be much less prone to heart disease than the Irish. His observation has become known as the French Paradox, and it is still true today. For example, the rate of cardiovascular disease is almost three times as high in the USA as it is in France.

Many scientific studies point to red wine as the most important factor in the French Paradox. Part of the reason for this is the alcohol in the wine. Alcohol can lower cholesterol and decrease blood pressure. It also makes the blood platelets less "sticky," which makes clots less likely. Long-term studies show that moderate drinkers live longer and are less likely to have heart disease than both non-drinkers and heavy drinkers. And in several studies comparing drinkers of different types of alcoholic drink, red wine has consistently come out top.

In 2002, the World Health Organization's Technical Committee on Cardiovascular Disease stated that the link between moderate alcohol consumption and reduced numbers of deaths from heart disease could no longer be doubted. Daily consumption of one or two glasses of red wine reduces the risk of heart disease significantly.

How much alcohol?

You shouldn't assume that a glass of wine carries one unit of alcohol. This is only true of a 125 milliliter glass of wine at 8 percent alcohol by volume (ABV).

To work out how many units of alcohol are in an alcoholic drink: multiply the volume of drink in milliliters by percentage ABV and divide by 1,000.

Attempts to find out exactly how red wine might play a part in protecting us from heart disease have highlighted tantalizing possibilities. Several studies have shown that the flavonoids in red wine reduce the body's production of a chemical called endothelin-1, which is made in the lining of our arteries. Make less of it and your risk of heart disease goes down.

So often, things that we like to eat or drink are bad for our health, and vice versa. Red wine, in moderation, is a welcome exception. So go on, drink to your health.

TOP TIPS – Red wine for your heart

Drink a glass of red wine with your evening meal. Remember, a unit of alcohol is a small glass (125ml) of 8 percent ABV wine – most home-poured drinks are larger and stronger.

The recommendations for alcohol intake are no more than 2–3 units per day for women and 3–4 units per day for men, preferably with one or two alcohol-free days a week.

Alternatively, for an alcohol-free procyanidin fix, try:

Food	Portion (equivalent to an average procyanidin content of a 125ml glass of red wine)
Dark chocolate	One square (about 6–7g)
Cranberry juice	A small glass (about 200ml)
Apple (Granny Smiths and Red Delicious)	A quarter of an apple (about 25g)

Procyanidins belong to a family of compounds called polyphenols. These compounds are of great interest because of the association between their consumption and health.

The best wines for polyphenol content are made with hardy grapes grown at high altitude. An example is South American Cabernet Sauvignon wines. Wines made by the traditional slow method also have a higher polyphenol content.

Tomatoes:
saving your skin

Sun worshippers beware: sitting in the sun for too long really can make your skin age faster. Ultraviolet radiation in sunlight is the single biggest factor in skin aging, even for smokers. And you don't have to sunbathe religiously to be affected. Everyday exposure to sunlight causes most of the damage.

Your skin is the largest organ of your body – and it is the only one that most people see. We're all getting older, but most of us would rather postpone the inevitable wrinkles, the deep furrows and the pigment spots that betray our age. And it's not only vanity that makes us want to keep our skin looking young: a young-looking skin is a healthy skin.

In the battle to fight skin aging, the humble tomato is on your side – all day, every day.

Tomatoes

Ah, the tomato. Quintessentially summer. Still warm, picked straight from the vine on a lazy Mediterranean afternoon. Juices dribbling down your chin when you take that first bite. Or plump and piled high on market stalls, proud alongside the strings of garlic and bunches of fresh basil. In steaming soup to take away the chill of a winter's evening. Or saucy, smothered on to pizza bases, mingling with mozzarella. The tomato is a most versatile vegetable.

Or should that be "fruit"? In 1893, the US Supreme Court considered the case of a fruit importer who was being charged import duty on tomatoes at a time when duty was only payable on vegetables, not fruits. The court decided against the man, ruling that tomatoes are vegetables, and the decision has stuck. Actually, we probably think of tomatoes as vegetables because we use them as vegetables. But botanists classify tomatoes as fruit, because they're the ripened, seed-containing ovaries of flowers.

In order to maximize color and flavor, it is best to leave tomatoes on the vine to ripen. But ripe tomatoes are soft and can become damaged in transit. So the imported tomatoes sold in supermarkets are picked early, when they are green and firm. When they reach the UK they are treated with ethylene – a plant hormone that encourages ripening.

Most tomatoes produced in the UK are grown hydroponically – without soil – under carefully controlled conditions to maximize growth rates. They are also bred for their regular shape and size rather than their taste. The net result is that supermarket tomatoes can be less juicy and more insipid than locally grown, vine-ripened tomatoes.

Tomatoes owe their vivid color to a pigment called lycopene, which is present in ripe tomatoes irrespective of whether they have ripened naturally or artificially. Lycopene has created quite a stir in nutritional circles. One of the most exciting areas of research shows how it might protect your skin against sunlight and help keep it young.

Old skin

As we age, our skin becomes increasingly dry, thin, saggy and wrinkled. It becomes dotted with irregular patches of pigment. Older skin also bruises more easily and is at greater risk of diseases, including skin cancers.

You only have to look at someone who spends most of their time outside to see the effects of sunlight on skin. The classic "weather-beaten" look of farmers and sailors is a result of accelerated skin aging due to long-term overexposure to the ultraviolet radiation in sunlight.

The huge range of sun protection lotions on the market can reduce the effects of ultraviolet radiation on your skin and help it stay younger longer. Tomatoes' special ingredient, lycopene, works in the same way. You don't have to slap it on like sun lotion. It is a built-in sunblock system that you carry around with you wherever you go and that protects you all over –

even when you're completely naked. What's more, it is completely natural and will offer protection all year round, not just on sunny, sunbathing days.

Raw tomatoes contain plenty of lycopene – as do papaya and pink grapefruit. But cooking tomatoes in a little oil can increase the availability of this wonderful chemical. There are two reasons for this. First of all, when you cook tomatoes you break down the cell walls, releasing the lycopene. Second, lycopene dissolves in fat and not in water. Tomato sauces – even ketchup – are great lycopene providers.

The tomato factor

Sunscreen lotions that you smear on your body work by reducing the amount of ultraviolet radiation that reaches your skin. The "sun protection factor" is an indication of how much ultraviolet they block. Factor 10 blocks 90 percent of ultraviolet, while factor 30 blocks nearly 97 percent.

Chemicals in sunscreen either reflect or absorb ultraviolet radiation. Lycopene – the natural sunscreen found in tomatoes – falls into the second category. It eats ultraviolet for breakfast – al fresco, of course.

When ultraviolet radiation hits the skin, it can have a variety of effects. On the positive side, it triggers the synthesis of vitamin D. This important chemical is found in oily fish and a few other foods. Vitamin D deficiency leads directly to rickets and osteoporosis, and is a contributing factor in several other diseases.

A fair-skinned person can synthesize a great deal of vitamin D by sitting in full sunshine for just a few minutes. Dark-skinned people produce much less than fair-skinned people. This is because their skin contains more melanin pigment, which blocks ultraviolet – in the same way as lycopene.

So dark-skinned people are at higher risk of diseases related to vitamin D deficiency than fair-skinned people, especially during the winter. However, the melanin is normally more of a benefit than a burden.

Dark-skinned people suffer less from the negative effects of ultraviolet on the skin, of which there are many. For example, ultraviolet radiation can break collagen – the strong, fibrous substance that holds our skin tight and flexible. It is damage to collagen – through normal aging and ultraviolet damage – that results in wrinkled, saggy skin.

Ultraviolet also damages DNA – the ultimate "molecule of life" found at the core of most cells in your body. Cancer results from damaged DNA, and ultraviolet damage to DNA in skin cells is the main cause of skin cancer.

By absorbing ultraviolet radiation, lycopene prevents some of the damage to DNA and collagen. But lycopene is also an antioxidant: it can help to mop up the free radicals that ultraviolet produces. Free radicals interfere with the proper functioning of the cell. For example, they too can damage DNA and they can break down the cell membrane.

The body has its own DNA repair molecules but if intense ultraviolet shines on your skin for an extended period, the damage is too much for them to cope with. Other molecules then raise the alarm, initiating a series of events that increase the blood supply to the area and cause the reddening called erythema. This is the first sign of sunburn – appearing just before the desire to sit in a bath of ice. So melanin gives dark-skinned people built-in protection against sunburn. And, studies show, lycopene can do the same even for those with fairer skin.

Tomato catch-up

Lycopene and tomatoes hit the headlines in 1995. In that year, Edward Giovannucci at the Harvard School of Public Health in the USA announced the results of a long-term study suggesting that eating lots of tomato products reduces men's chances of getting prostate cancer. In the same year, Judy Ribaya-Mercado at Tufts University in Boston published a study showing that ultraviolet destroys lycopene in skin. That makes sense because lycopene is a martyr: in the act of mopping up free radicals, it sacrifices itself. The body cannot make this wonderful chemical, so the message seems to be "eat lots of tomatoes."

Because lycopene is soluble in fat, it accumulates in several organs of the body – most notably the liver, lungs and prostate. Recent studies have suggested that a lycopene-rich diet reduces the risk of a number of serious diseases in these organs, and can help avoid coronary heart disease.

One unusual study indicates that lycopene might help you to live longer, not just age more slowly. It was part of a huge research program called the Nun Study, run by the US National Institute on Aging. The study involved ninety-four nuns – all aged between seventy-seven and ninety-nine and living in the same

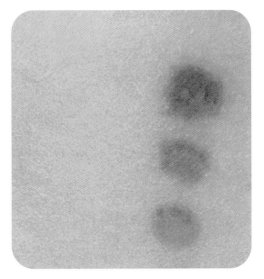

These two photos were taken during our experiment. The image on the left shows the skin on the buttocks of one of our volunteers after receiving a dose of ultraviolet radiation. The redness is caused by the inflammatory response that is the beginning of sunburn, or erythema. There is much less redness in the photograph on the right, which was taken at the end of the study, and shows a different patch of skin on the same buttock, which had received the same dose of ultraviolet radiation.

convent. The researchers measured the levels of lycopene in the nuns' blood over a period of six years. They found that 70 percent of the nuns with high levels of lycopene were still alive at the end of the study, while only 13 percent of those with low levels survived.

Many doctors and researchers view these results as encouraging. However, they are keen to point out that the findings have yet to be proven beyond doubt, partly to discourage people from taking lycopene supplements in pill form. As with many dietary supplement tablets, it is unknown whether the benefits of taking lycopene in tablets will match those from eating the real thing. Furthermore, tablets containing concentrated lycopene are expensive – and they don't taste as good as tomato sauce.

The science test

Lycopene is tomatoes' built-in sunblock that protects their skins from ultraviolet radiation in sunlight. Can you benefit from it if you eat tomatoes? We set out to test of the effects of lycopene in tomato sauce. We worked with Dr. Lesley Rhodes, Senior Lecturer in Dermatology at the University of Manchester and Mark Birch-Machin, Professor of Molecular Dermatology at Newcastle University. We found twenty-three female volunteers aged between twenty and fifty. None of the women had particularly sensitive skin, and none smoked.

We divided our volunteers into two groups. The first group received daily portions of tomato paste (55 grams), containing about 16 milligrams of lycopene, mixed with 10 grams of olive oil. The second group's daily portions were just the 10 grams of olive oil. The participants included their portions into their regular diets.

At the beginning of the experiment, and again at the end, we irradiated patches of skin on the women's buttocks with ultraviolet radiation. We assessed the effect of the radiation by measuring the amount of sunburn (erythema) it caused. To do this, we used a device called an erythema meter, which measures the color of the skin. We also measured the effect of the radiation at a molecular level, using a sophisticated technique that measured damage done to DNA in the skin cells.

The analysis of DNA damage was not completed in time to go into this book. But the amount of sunburn produced had more than halved following intake of the tomato paste. Our experts told us that there was a definite and marked improvement in the skin protection, which really did appear to be a result of the lycopene in the diet.

As with so many things in life, looking after your skin is a question of balance. Too much sunscreen and your body may not make enough vitamin D. Too little and you are at risk of skin cancer and premature aging. However you manage your intake of sunlight, it is certainly worth maintaining your intake of tomatoes.

TOP TIPS – Lycopene for the skin

If you want to try the same diet that the volunteers were given in the study, you need to eat 16mg of lycopene every day, which you would get from eating one of the following:

Food	Portion
Tomato paste	55g (about 3 dessert spoonfuls)
Fresh raw tomatoes	600g (7–8 medium sized tomatoes)
Canned tomato soup	300ml (small mug or bowl)
Tomato juice	200ml (small glass)
Canned tomatoes	400g (about 1 can)
Sun dried tomatoes	40g
Tomato sauce	100ml (6–7 tablespoons)

Cooking and processing (e.g. chopping finely) helps to improve the absorption of lycopene. So does adding a little oil.

Can't stand tomatoes? Try these foods for similar lycopene content:

Food	Portion
Red grapefruit	3 grapefruits
Guava juice	300ml (an average glass)
Watermelon	350g (about ¼ melon)

Water:
how much is not enough?

In 2005, the BBC's website carried a survey that asked the question: "Do you think we need to drink two liters of water every day?" More than 90 percent answered "yes" to this question. How would you answer?

Water "slaves" are everywhere. They carry bottles of mineral water wherever they go, and they swig and gulp all day, desperate to ensure that they drink their two liters. They are not allowed to include cups of coffee or tea, nor the water in their food. And they do this because so many nutrition gurus in the health columns of magazines and newspapers tell them it is absolutely essential. They explain that drinking this much water will not only save us from dehydration, it will rejuvenate our skin, make our hair shine, and detoxify our whole bodies.

In reality, the idea that we all need to drink two liters of water every day is a myth. Most of us don't need this much water to avoid dehydration. Furthermore, when we do calculate our daily intake of water, it is fine to include the water in coffee and tea – and in our food. And drinking more water will not flush out toxins or rejuvenate our skin or our hair.

Water – the inside story

Although water has no nutritional value, it is absolutely essential. Each of the 100 billion or so cells of your body is mostly water. Then there are the fluids filling the spaces between the cells, and finally the watery bloodstream. Altogether, we are two-thirds water – that's more than 40 liters in an adult of average weight. If you lost just 5 percent of your body's water content, you would be in a state of extreme dehydration. Your mind would become confused, your body very weak. Eventually, of course, you would die. You can live without food for about ten days or more, but without water, you would die after just two.

The opposite of dehydration is water intoxication. It can lead to an irregular heartbeat, fluttering eyelids, and behaviors similar to being drunk. Water intoxication can also cause death. Maintaining the correct amount of water in your body is clearly a very important job.

When you drink water, you take in billions and billions of water molecules with each gulp. When you eat food, you are usually eating plant or animal cells. Each of these cells is mostly water, encapsulated in the cell membrane, and with various chemicals dissolved in it. Even toast and crackers contain some water. After you have eaten or drunk something, you absorb water molecules through the wall of your intestines. You also gain at least 250 milliliters each day as a by-product of chemical reactions in your cells.

Science fact

Each water molecule is made of two hydrogen atoms and one oxygen atom. This gives the familiar chemical formula H_2O. The shape of the molecule is reminiscent of a silhouette of Mickey Mouse: the large oxygen atom is the head and the hydrogens are the ears.

You need to take in water to replace what your body loses. Some goes down the toilet, some is released into the air as water vapor when you breathe out, and some leaves your body through the pores in your skin. How much you lose depends upon how active you are and the temperature and humidity of the air around you.

Maintaining balance

Crucially, the amount of water you lose depends on another factor: your current state of hydration. On a day when you don't lose a huge amount through sweating, you will lose at least 1.3 liters of water – and as much as 20 liters if it's hot and you're really exerting yourself. Drink lots of water on a normal day and you will lose

lots of water. In that case, your urine will be very pale yellow or almost completely clear. If you are not taking in very much, your body will retain as much as it can. Your urine will be darker yellow.

Your body's built-in water regulation system works automatically, day and night. It works by monitoring how concentrated or diluted your fluids are. If you are lacking water, so that your fluids are a little more concentrated than usual, your body produces a hormone called vasopressin. This hormone affects your kidneys, which is where your urine is prepared. It makes the kidneys retain water, so that your urine becomes more concentrated. Importantly, your body's dilution monitors also send messages to your brain, making you feel thirsty. If your fluids are diluted enough – or too diluted – your body stops producing vasopressin, your kidneys start making more watered-down urine, and you stop feeling thirsty.

The sensation of thirst is powerful and kicks in when we have lost 1 or 2 percent of our total body water. This is long before we can be called dehydrated. Providing you have access to water, it is unlikely that you will become severely dehydrated – your body won't let you.

Watery truth

The body's system of water regulation works very well in normal circumstances. It seems likely that if we were not drinking enough water, we would soon know about it. The large proportion of the population who drink less than two liters of pure water each day would all feel very thirsty all the time. They would at least notice the color of their urine grow alarmingly darker day by day.

Research backs up the common-sense suggestion that – for healthy people at least – eight glasses of water every day is not really

necessary. In one study, for example, urine from people who had drunk differing amounts of water showed no difference in the total amounts of "toxic" substances – or even unwanted but harmless ones. The body gets rid of what it can in urine, but drinking more simply makes the urine more diluted – it does not take more with it.

So what about caffeinated drinks and alcohol? Is it true that coffee, tea and alcohol are "diuretics," boosting urine production? Does drinking them actually result in a net loss of water? Several careful studies have shown that coffee and caffeinated soft drinks have no significant effect on urine production at all. In other words, drinking a cup of coffee has more or less the same effect as drinking a cup of water. So you can safely include caffeinated drinks in working out your daily fluid intake.

The only drinks that can produce a net loss of water are alcoholic ones, and even then only if you drink several glasses. Alcohol blocks the production of vasopressin, so the body reacts as if it has too much water, and produces lots of diluted urine. The headache you can experience after a heavy intake of alcohol is largely due to dehydration. You are unlikely to suffer any long-term effects – from the dehydration at least.

In 2002, Dr. Heinz Valtin of the Dartmouth Medical School in New Hampshire, USA, uncovered the likely source of the "2 liters a day" recommendation. Valtin has worked for more than forty years researching the body's water regulation systems. He believes that the advice comes from a misinterpretation of a 1945 report by the US Food and Nutrition Board. A key part of the report explains that the body needs about one milliliter of water to process each calorie that it consumes. The average diet is 2,000 calories per day, which suggests a daily intake of two liters of water. However, the report states that "most of this is contained in prepared foods" – something that the modern water myth overlooks.

Body of water

Although the suggestion that we should all drink two liters of water a day is a myth, there are some people who are advised to drink water whether their bodies are telling them to or not. They include people with certain medical conditions – for example, kidney stones – and elderly people, whose bodies' own mechanisms for water regulation do not work as well as they used to.

There are some people for whom two liters every day might be too much. Some people with diabetes take vasopressin in tablet form, for example. They would not be able to excrete excess water in their urine, and they might become water-intoxicated. Careful water management is essential for these people.

Of course, keeping yourself properly hydrated is vital. Constant mild dehydration can affect your salivary glands, encourage the growth of kidney stones and make you feel tired. But the truth about water is that most of us are getting just what we need. Many of us are probably drinking a little more than we need – and visiting the toilet a little more often as a result. For some very active people, or on hot, dry days, two liters may not be enough. In those cases, you will feel dry and thirsty. Drink something or eat something moist and your body will absorb the water it needs. The bottom line is that we should not take a "one size fits all" approach to water consumption.

The science test

Having been convinced that most of the population are not severely dehydrated, we wondered about the effects of water consumption on skin and hair. Can drinking more water make your skin and hair look and feel rejuvenated? The science behind your body's water-regulation system would suggest not. You can't force extra water into skin cells to plump them up, for example. To find out the truth – and to convince the unbelievers – we decided to put it to the test.

Sisters Susie and Alice both adhered strictly to the two-liter rule. They both lead busy lives, going to work, socializing and occasionally working out at the gym. We asked Susie to abstain from her water habit for five days. During those five days, we made sure the women ate and drank the same – apart from the extra two liters of water drunk by Alice each day.

Before and after those five days, we used a "Triplesense" sensor to measure the women's skin moisture content and elasticity. We also looked at their skin close up, using a sophisticated confocal microscope that can produce stunning cross-sectional images of details one-thousandth of a millimeter across. And we measured the color of the women's urine, to gauge their levels of hydration.

The tests at the beginning and the end of the experiment showed that neither sister was dehydrated. Both sisters' skin was in great condition in both tests. The only difference was that Alice had had to buy an expensive two-liter bottle of mineral water every day for five days. And she probably spent more time in the toilet.

The water myth

Despite what you hear in newspapers and magazines, you don't necessarily need two liters of water every day. Your body will tell you to take some more fluids on board long before you become dehydrated – and caffeinated and alcoholic drinks, and the water in food, do contribute to your total intake for the day.

TRUTH ABOUT FOOD NO. 11:
MOST PEOPLE DON'T NEED TO DRINK TWO LITRES OF WATER EVERY DAY – AND COFFEE, TEA AND ALCOHOLIC DRINKS DO COUNT TOWARD YOUR FLUID INTAKE.

TRUTH ABOUT FOOD NO. 12:

TOMATO SKINS ARE A GREAT SOURCE OF LYCOPENE, A CHEMICAL THAT HELPS PREVENT SKIN CANCER.

THE TRUTH ABOUT FOOD

Spinach:
vision for the future?

Eyesight is one of those precious things that it is easy to take for granted – until, perhaps, it's too late. As the rest of the body ages, our eyes age, too. But recent scientific findings suggest that certain foods can help to protect eyes against age-related damage – and spinach is one of the best.

Spinach has a strange reputation. Children tend to hate it. But like broccoli and sprouts many parents feel an obligation to encourage their children to eat it. In days gone by, it was usually enthusiastically overcooked and served as a sloppy mess. In that form, it leaves a weird slimy taste in your mouth. It was something to be avoided at all costs.

Nowadays, the deep green leaves of the spinach plant have had something of a rebirth for many people. It is a wonderful vegetable and a quick blitz in a heavy pan with a drop of water preserves both its flavor and texture. It has also become a highly desirable raw ingredient and the tender baby leaves are a permanent fixture in many families' salads.

Most people have a dim memory that spinach contains a lot of iron, but some people say that is just a myth. Some people say it's not really that good for us at all. So what is the truth about spinach? And can it really help to save people's sight?

Lean and green

Like all leafy green vegetables, spinach is very nutritious. It contains no fat but plenty of dietary fiber, antioxidants, and a good supply of vitamins and minerals. One of the important vitamins is folic acid (vitamin B9). Many mothers will recognize that name because doctors recommend eating foods rich in folic acid during pregnancy, to reduce their own risk of anemia and their baby's risk of being born with serious birth defects.

After spinach is picked, the amounts of folic acid and antioxidants it contains quickly begin to decrease. So if you buy fresh spinach, it is important to eat it within a few days – perhaps up to eight days if you keep it refrigerated.

Washed spinach can go annoyingly limp and rotten-looking in the fridge, however. To avoid this, dry it thoroughly in a salad spinner and put it loose into an open bag in the salad drawer of the fridge. If you don't like it raw, bear in mind that boiling spinach for more than about four minutes destroys nearly all the folic acid. So if you are going to cook it, steaming is better.

Spinach was first cultivated in ancient Persia (now Iran). It was introduced to Europe about 700 years ago and became popular during the 1600s. But its heyday was in the 1930s when it was hailed as a wonder food, mainly because of its supposedly high iron content. The cartoon character Popeye, who acquires super-human strength when he eats spinach, made his first appearance in 1929 and his popularity caused a 30 percent increase in spinach consumption in the USA during the 1930s.

In 1937, German chemists uncovered an unfortunate error: the supposed concentration of iron in spinach was off by a factor of ten because of a simple miscalculation nearly sixty years earlier. Actually, for a vegetable spinach does contain a good deal of iron, but our bodies cannot absorb much of it. Most of the iron combines with a chemical called oxalic acid, also plentiful in spinach. The resulting compound is indigestible, so that most of the iron passes straight through us.

Spinach consumption may increase once again in the coming years, though not as a result of a cartoon character. It may be science that does it this time. Experiments have shown that eating spinach can help to prevent a debilitating eye disease called age-related macular degeneration. There are no spectacles that can correct the effects of this disease, and there is no known cure. That should be enough to encourage anyone who values their eyesight to eat their greens.

Distorted view

Age-related macular degeneration (AMD) is the result of damage to cells in the retina, the inner surface at the back of the eye. The retina is the part of the eye where light forms an image – just like the image inside a camera. It contains millions of light-sensitive cells, which send signals to the brain. Free radicals damage the cells of the retina and put some out of action altogether – just as they do to cells elsewhere in the body. The most important cells are also the ones most at risk. They are found in the central part of the retina, the macula, which helps us to see fine detail.

One out of every six people over sixty suffers from AMD. By the age of seventy-five, about one in three has it. AMD does not make you lose your sight completely, but it disrupts your vision so much that many sufferers are considered "legally blind." In fact, it is the leading cause of legal blindness in the developed world. An estimated 17 million Americans have AMD and about 2 million of them are legally blind as a result. In the UK, about 770,000 people have the disease.

One cruel side effect of the damage that AMD causes is that debris from dead cells builds up underneath the retina, making it bumpy. This distorts the image the eye sees. So AMD sufferers often have partial blindness right at the center of their vision, with severely distorted vision elsewhere. And all of this is because of damage caused by free radicals in the macula.

Harsh light

Unfortunately, exposure to light itself produces free radicals in the retina. So unless you wear a blindfold all day long, some damage is inevitable.

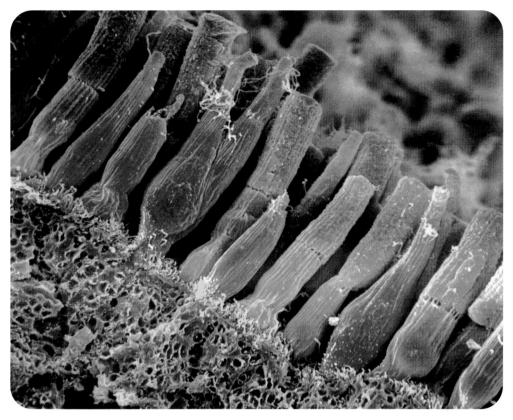

This remarkable false-color image shows the light-sensitive cells of a human retina. It was captured using a scanning electron microscope. Light strikes from the top. Rod cells (green) are sensitive only to light and dark; cone cells (blue) allow us to see in color. Beneath these cells is a layer that contains pigment, which absorbs light. In the macula, the thickest part of the retina, there is lots of protective pigment.

The brighter the light, and the bluer the light, the more free radicals are produced. Ultraviolet is the most destructive. Of course, nature has a way of protecting the eyes. Spread throughout the retina is a pigment that absorbs blue light and ultraviolet. This pigment is like the eye's built-in sunglasses, blocking much of the ultraviolet before it can do any harm.

The pigment in the retina has another role: it is a potent antioxidant. So when potentially damaging free radicals do crop up in the cells of the retina, they are often stopped in their tracks before they can do any harm. The protective pigment of the retina is concentrated in the macula, where it is needed most. Scientists normally refer to it as "macular pigment" and if you have less than you need, you are in danger of developing AMD.

Amazingly, our bodies cannot manufacture macular pigment. It is composed of two yellow-orange chemical compounds that are only made in plants. So the only way we can maintain levels of the pigment in our eyes is by making sure we eat foods that contain it. The two chemicals in macular pigment go by the exotic names of lutein and zeaxanthin, and the best sources are leafy green vegetables and sweetcorn. Egg yolk is another good dietary source of lutein and zeaxanthin – the more of these compounds in a hen's diet, the more yellow her yolks will be.

Analysis of human eyes has shown that, not surprisingly, people with AMD have less macular pigment than those who do not. It thins out with age, which is why the disease is age-related. Several studies have shown that a diet rich in foods that contain lutein and zeaxanthin can reduce the risk of AMD significantly. Some studies have suggested that people who already have the disease can ease their symptoms simply by increasing their intake of leafy vegetables.

Kale is the best leafy green source of lutein and zeaxanthin, but spinach is much more popular and versatile. A recent poll rated it the eighth most popular vegetable in Britain. And so spinach, rather than kale, has featured in many of the research projects concerning eye health. We wanted to investigate the possible link between spinach and AMD for ourselves, so we carried out our own experiment and got some pretty impressive results. You may never look at spinach in quite the same way again.

The science test

It is a fairly straightforward idea: spinach contains pigments that help protect the eye, that our bodies cannot produce, and that need replenishing as we grow older. So, eat more spinach and you will remain protected for longer. Sounds too good to be true. Can it really work? Previous studies have shown that lutein in capsule form can increase the concentration of macular pigment – we wanted to see if lutein in spinach could do the same.

We enlisted two scientists two help us plan and carry out the study. They were Dr. Neil Parry, from the Vision Science Centre at the Manchester Eye Hospital and Dr. Ian Murray, Senior Lecturer at Manchester University's Faculty of Life Sciences, who has carried out previous studies into the effects of diet on macular pigment.

We decided to treat twelve volunteers to three months of a spinach-rich diet (not everyone's idea of heaven). At the outset, we used sophisticated "fundus" photography to produce detailed pictures of the participants' retinas. The fundus is the name for the entire back surface inside the eye, which includes the retina. A technique called flicker photometry was used to measure the thickness of their macular pigment.

Every day for twelve weeks, our volunteers ate 50 grams of spinach, which contains about 10 milligrams of lutein. The pigment is best absorbed when some kind of fat is eaten at the same time. So spinach pies are OK, spinach on pizza is fine. We supplied our volunteers with olive oil to include with their daily spinach intake. We also gave them a wide selection of suitable recipes. At the end of the twelve weeks, we carried out the same tests on our volunteers, to see if anything had changed. Could nearly three months of eating spinach have been for nothing?

Although the experiment was complete, the full results were not in by the time this book went to print. There appeared to be definite improvement in the thickness of the macular pigment in the retinas of our volunteers. Spinach, it seems, really is more than just something sloppy sent to make children miserable. Carry on eating it into adulthood, and it could just save your sight.

TOP TIPS – Spinach for the eyes

Here's how to eat the same amount of lutein that the volunteers were given in the study.

Every day eat one of the following:

Food	Portion
Spinach	50g steamed (about ¼ a bag)
Kale	30g steamed (1 large tablespoon)

Or you could try the following, generous portion sizes!

Peas	250g (about 7 tablespoons)
Summer squash	350g (about 9 tablespoons)
Brussels sprouts	500g (about 50 sprouts)
Pumpkin	500g (about 12 tablespoons)
Broccoli	Raw or cooked: 350g (one small bunch)

Lutein is absorbed more efficiently with a little fat, so add a tiny knob of butter to cooked vegetables, or a vegetable-based spread.

SUMMARY: HOW TO STAY YOUNG AND BEAUTIFUL

 A REGULAR INTAKE OF BERRIES AND OTHER FRUITS AND VEGETABLES CAN HELP KEEP YOUR BRAIN YOUNG.

The rumor seems to be true: red wine contains chemical compounds that reduce your chances of heart disease – when it is drunk in moderation of course.

THERE IS A CHEMICAL IN TOMATO SKINS, WHICH IS ALSO FOUND IN WATERMELONS, GUAVA AND RED GRAPEFRUIT, THAT ACTS AS A NATURAL SUNSCREEN, HELPING TO KEEP YOUR SKIN YOUNGER FOR LONGER.

The idea that everyone should drink two liters of water every day is a myth; the amount of water your body needs depends on many factors, and your natural thirst mechanism kicks in long before you are dehydrated.

 Spinach is a great source of pigments that protect the retina; they can help protect your eyes from damage and, in particular, a disease called age-related macular degeneration.

GLOSSARY

antioxidant (nutritional) – a chemical that slows down a type of chemical reaction called oxidation, which can cause damage inside the body. Examples are the vitamins A and C, and the mineral selenium. Antioxidants are essential in the fight against cancer and aging. See free radical.

antioxidant (food additive) – you sometimes see antioxidants listed in the ingredients on the labels of processed food. They are added to help make the food stay fresh for longer – they are not necessarily beneficial to your health.

bile – a greenish liquid made by the liver, and stored in the gall bladder between meals. During digestion, bile leaks into the small intestine, where it helps to break up fat globules.

calorie (cal) – a unit of energy, the one most often used when dealing with food. When people say "calorie," they normally mean "kilocalorie." So, if someone tells you a chocolate bar has 200 calories, it actually has 200 kilocalories (200,000 calories).

carbohydrate – any chemical compound made up of the elements carbon, hydrogen and oxygen and no other elements. Sugars, starch and dietary fiber are examples of carbohydrates. Those that can be digested are used by the body to provide energy.

cholesterol – a soft, waxy substance that plays an essential role in many body processes. In the blood, it is carried in globules called lipoproteins. A high level of one form of lipoprotein (called low-density lipoprotein, or LDL) is associated with an increased risk of heart disease and stroke. LDL is often called "bad cholesterol," while the other main lipoprotein, high-density lipoprotein (HDL), is often called "good cholesterol," because it is not associated with health problems.

DNA – stands for deoxyribonucleic acid; often referred to as the molecule of life. It carries information from generation to generation, and acts as a blueprint and template for building your body.

enzyme – a type of protein that plays a part in important chemical reactions inside living things. There are digestive enzymes, for example, which help to break down large, complex molecules in food into small, simple molecules that can be absorbed into the body.

fat – one of the macronutrients (along with carbohydrates and proteins). It accumulates in fat cells, most of which are just under the skin and around your internal organs. Fat provides insulation and shock absorption. Your body manufactures fat, as an energy store, if you take in more calories than you use up.

fiber – any indigestible carbohydrate, such as cellulose found in plants. It absorbs water as it passes through your digestive system, preventing your feces from being too dry. Some fiber feeds beneficial bacteria in your large intestine. A high-fiber diet has many health benefits.

free radical – a chemical that easily takes part in chemical reactions. Inside your body, free radicals can damage your cells, contributing to aging. See antioxidant.

glucose – a simple sugar that is the body's main ready supply of energy. When you eat foods with carbohydrates in them, the carbohydrates break down in your digestive system to form glucose, which is absorbed into your blood.

glycogen – a chemical compound similar to glucose, and formed from glucose inside cells in the liver and muscles. When there is more than enough glucose in the blood, the excess is stored away as glycogen; when there is not enough, the glycogen forms glucose again, and is released into the blood.

glycemic index (GI) – a measure of how quickly a carbohydrate-rich food increases your blood sugar concentration. Pure glucose, which dissolves rapidly into the blood, is used as a reference, with a GI of 100. Low GI foods, which release glucose slowly, include apple juice and pasta.

HDL (high-density lipoprotein) – see cholesterol.

insulin – a hormone produced by the pancreas, and released into the blood when the concentration of blood sugar rises after a meal. It causes cells to absorb glucose.

kilocalorie (kcal) – see calorie.

LDL (low-density lipoprotein) – see cholesterol.

macronutrient – any of the three most important families of substance in food: carbohydrates, fats and proteins.

metabolic rate – the rate at which the body uses energy, usually expressed as kilocalories per day.

micronutrient – any important chemical compound in foods that is not a carbohydrate, fat, protein, water or fiber. Vitamins, minerals and antioxidants are examples of micronutrients.

mineral – chemical element essential in our diets (except carbon, hydrogen, nitrogen and oxygen, which are found in abundance in all foods). Most dietary minerals are metals; examples include iron and calcium.

monounsaturated fat – a type of unsaturated fat found in some foods, including olive oil and sesame oil.

polyunsaturated fat – a type of unsaturated fat found in some foods, including mayonnaise, sunflower oil and oily fish, and generally regarded as a healthy type of fat. Omega-3 and omega-6 fatty acids are polyunsaturated fats.

protein – one of the macronutrients (along with carbohydrates and fats). Digestive enzymes break down proteins into smaller molecules called amino acids. Inside your body's cells, amino acids join together to make new protein molecules. Proteins make up about half the dry weight of every cell in your body; enzymes are proteins, and hair and nails are almost pure protein.

saturated fat – a type of fat found commonly in meat, cheese and butter, and generally regarded as unhealthy in large quantities. The consumption of high levels of saturated fat is associated with heart disease.

starch – a carbohydrate common in many foods, including bread, rice and potatoes. It breaks down easily to form glucose. Plants make starch as a way of storing glucose – it is the plant equivalent of glycogen.

trans fats – a type of fat normally made by reacting vegetable oil with hydrogen (they are then called partially-hydrogenated vegetable oils). Trans fats are soft, and ideal for baking, and they do not spoil as quickly as vegetable oils. They are found in fast foods and confectionery, although they are becoming less common, because they are the least healthy type of fat. Trans fat in your diet increases your risk of developing heart disease.

unsaturated fat – a type of fat that is most often found in fish and vegetables, and is regarded as healthier than saturated fats.

vitamin – a micronutrient essential to the human body, and found in food (in particular, in fruits and vegetables). Some vitamins are antioxidants, others take part in important chemical reactions. A deficiency of each vitamin causes disease; for example, if you do not eat enough vitamin C, you will develop a disease called scurvy; lack of vitamin D can lead to rickets.

ACKNOWLEDGMENTS

This book would not have been possible without the vision, commitment and enthusiastic support of many institutions and individuals. First and foremost I would like to thank over 500 volunteers who took part in *The Truth About Food* television series to discover how food affected their bodies. My thanks too, to Fiona Bruce, Colin Jackson, Jan Ravens, Jim Moir (Vic Reeves), Liza Tarbuck and Andrea Oliver for their willingness to take risks on this project. They were always enthusiastic and gave the series that indefinable star quality.

Thanks to all those in BBC Television who have been involved with the films: Emma Swain who commissioned the series and believed in it from the outset; John Lynch, Head of Science and History, with whom I have worked for many years, whose advice I have always valued and who is now a personal friend. In the States, Toni Egger from Discovery Channel, who helped frame the series, Alon Orstein our Executive Producer and Donald Thoms, the Vice President of Production. Thanks too to Regine Beutel from the ProSeiben Channel in Germany for all her dedication and hard work.

A huge thanks also to the entire *The Truth About Food* production team (listed below), whose energy, talent and enthusiasm made the series such a pleasure to make. The television series has been enormously important in forming the ideas for this book and I particularly want to thank Alice Harper, an outstanding and talented Series Producer whose passion and commitment to the series never wavered. Together with her team, including Liz Biggs, Katie Lobban, Clare Mottershead, Penny Palmer, Nicky Shale and Catherine Verity, we created content that became worthy of this book. Thanks, too, to a wonderful researcher, Lucy Smith, for her unflinching, wise and informed criticisms.

The Top Tips were developed in collaboration with scientists at the Medical Research Council, Human Nutrition Research, apart from those in Chapter 5, which were developed by sports dietician Jane Griffin. Thanks also to the following:

How to be healthy:
Professor Tom Sanders, Professor of Nutrition and Dietetics at Kings College London; Lynne Garton from Alimenta; Dr. Mark McAlindon, University of Nottingham; Professor Glenn Gibson and one of his research students, Gemma Watson, the University of Reading; Professor Alan Boobis, Professor Martin Wilkins and Emily Russell from Hammersmith Hospital.

How to be slim:
Professor Robin Spiller and Dr. Luca Marciani at the Wolfson Digestive Diseases Centre, University of Nottingham; Professor Penny Gowland, Sir Peter Mansfield at Magnetic Resonance Centre, University of Nottingham; Mr. John Totman at the Brain and Body Centre, University of Nottingham; Dr. David McCarthy, Institute for Health Research and Policy, London Metropolitan University; Soren Brage and Kate Westgate, Medical Research Council, Human Nutrition Research Epidemiology Unit; Dr. Corby Martin, Instructor in Health Psychology, Pennington Research Center, Baton Rouge, Louisiana; Professor Arne Astrup (and two of his

research students, Nathalie Bendsen and Anne-Louise Hother Nielsen) Head of Human Nutrition Department, Royal Veterinary and Agricultural University, Copenhagen, Denmark; Professor Brian Wansink, Julian Simon Fellow and Professor of Marketing, Nutritional Science and Agricultural Economics at the University of Illinois; Dr. Susan Jebb, Dr. Toni Steer, Claire MacEvilly and Antony Wright, Medical Research Council, Human Nutrition Research.

How to feed the kids:

Professor David Benton, University of Swansea; Mr. Paul Sacher, MEND Research leader and nutritionist at Great Ormond Street Hospital, London; Professor Peter Hepper, Queen's University Belfast.

How to be sexy:

Dr. Allan Pacey and Fiona Ford, University of Sheffield; Dr. Graham Jackson and Dr. Alethea Cooper, Guy's and St. Thomas' Hospitals, London; Catherine Collins, St. George's Hospital, London; Peter Josling at the Garlic Institute; Nigel Denby; Dr. Nick Panay; Dr. Allan Hirsch, The Smell and Taste Treatment and Research Center, Chicago; Dr. Harry Witchel, University of Bristol.

How to be the best:

British Military Fitness, especially Crispin Vitoria and Jeremy Wormington; Professor Peter Rogers and Sue Heatherley from University of Bristol; Asker Jeukendrup, Birmingham University; Roger Harris, Chester Hill and Glenys Jones, University of Chichester; Dr. Brent Ruby and John Cuddy, University of Montana, Missoula; Alex Richardson at FAB Research and Oxford University, and Dr. Alan Watkins at Cardiac Coherence; Professor David Jones at University of Birmingham.

How to stay young and beautiful:

Dr. Lesley Rhodes, Dr. Muneeza Rizwan, Dr. Neil Parry, Dr. Ian Murray and Sue Ritchie from the University of Manchester.

Special thanks also to Patrick Walsh of the London literary agency Conville and Walsh, who is a great agent; also to the talented and calm Caz Hildebrand, who was the driving force behind the book and its design. My publishers, Bloomsbury Publishing, have been terrific and highly encouraging. Particular thanks to Mike Jones for his amazing backing and unstinting commitment to the project. The book could not have been completed in the time available to me without the solid work, insight and wisdom of Jack Challoner. His support has contributed more than he will ever acknowledge to this book.

My biggest debt as always is to my family: to my daughter Billie, my stepchildren Charlie, Alex, Michael and Corrina and my partner Andrew for his tolerance, good humor – and love.

***The Truth About Food* team:**

Executive Producer: Jill Fullerton-Smith

Series Producer: Alice Harper

Directors: Konrad Begg, Gideon Bradshaw, Adam Kaleta, Caroline Penry-Davey, Andy Devonshire, Nat Sharman, Libby Turner, Giles Harrison, Victoria Bell, Carney Turner.

Assistant Producers: Lucy Bailey, Liz Biggs, Liz Collier, Alison Draper, Jess Gilman, Katie Lobban, Clare Mottershead, Penny Palmer, Nicky Shale, Catherine Verity.

Researchers: Sarah Hunter, Will Ellerby, James McGhie.

Production Team: Alison Mills, Rebecca Lavender, Anna McGill, Sarah Casey, Juliane Hoffman, Claire Askew, Julie Wilkinson, Lucy Smith, Lisa Crow, Roisin McNeil, Jessica Brewster, Elizabeth Kargbo, Gemma Newby, Sophie Layen, Ella Gutteridge, Caroline Jagger, John O'Neill.

For more information, you can visit The Truth About Food website at

http://www.bbc.co.uk/truthaboutfood

INDEX